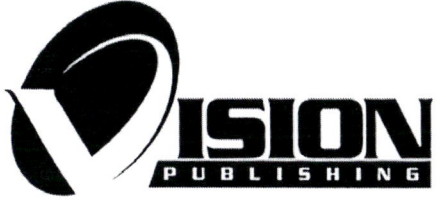

WINNING WAYS

How to Achieve Success...
No Matter What!

A'YANNA WEBSTER

Copyright © 2006 by A'Yanna T. Webster
All rights reserved. No part of this book may be used or reproduced in any form whatsoever without permission from the publisher. For more information contact:

Vision Publishing
P.O. Box 7237
Kansas City, MO 64113
www.thinkbigvision.com
1.888.98.VISION

An original publication of Vision Publishing
a division of Vision Marketing & Consulting, LLC
First Edition

ISBN 0-9774578-0-X
   1. Inspirational /Motivational

Editor: Q. Elizabeth Gibson
Cover Design: Gino L. Morrow II
Photography: Grady Bell

Library of Congress Cataloging Publication Data
Vision Publishing 2006
Printed in the U.S.A.

Dedication

    This book is dedicated to my beloved and departed family members who taught me so much about what it really means to be a success. My grandmother, Ella Mae Gilmore (1929-2003), and my uncle and aunt, Pastor Armour D. Stephenson, Jr. (1955-2005) and Pastor Shirley Stephenson, (1958-2005); three of the greatest examples I know of **How to Achieve Success**…*No Matter What!* I am eternally grateful for the exemplary lives they led.

Acknowledgments

First and foremost, I give thanks to my **Lord and Savior, Jesus Christ,** who is the author and finisher of my faith. Without Him I am nothing and can do nothing; with Him I can do ALL things.

To **my husband, Garrett-** my best friend, lover, coach, and business partner. Thank you for the love and support you've shown me throughout this process. Every woman should be as blessed as I am to have a husband like you.

To **my mother, Volean,** You've always taught me that I could do and become anything in this life that I set my heart and mind to. Guess what? You were right.

To **my family and friends-** who have supported me and continue to encourage me.

To **Cathy Coleman-** my friend and spiritual sister, thank you for your continued love, prayers, and words of encouragement.

To **my Pastor and First Lady, Bishop Mark and Sis. Emelda Tolbert-** thank you for being shining examples of success, not only in the spirit realm but in the natural as well.

To **the Christ Temple Church Family**, thank you for covering me in love and prayer.

To **all those who helped** in making the production of this book possible and most of all, **Vision Publishing**; to you I also say a heartfelt thank you.

Finally, to **YOU who will read this book**, I pray that God will grant you new and continued success in everything you do. Come what may; know that there IS a winner in you...**NO MATTER WHAT!**

Contents

FOREWARD i

INTRODUCTION iii

Week 1

Day	1	Begin with the End in Mind	1
Day	2	Go for the Goal	5
Day	3	Never Give Up	9
Day	4	Compete Against the Best…YOU	13
Day	5	Take Action	17
Day	6	Hard Work Is the Key	21
Day	7	Prioritize Your Life	25

Week 2

Day 8	Follow Your Heart's Desire	29
Day 9	Recognize Your Fears	33
Day 10	Overcome Obstacles	37
Day 11	Become a Daily Success	41
Day 12	Empower Yourself	45
Day 13	Ask Without Forgiveness	49
Day 14	Let Your Light Shine	53

Week 3

Day 15	Travel Light	57
Day 16	Put the Past Behind You	61

Day 17	Be Resilient	65
Day 18	Become Someone You've Never Been	69
Day 19	Do More	73
Day 20	Give More Than You Get	77
Day 21	Build a Support System	81

Week 4

Day 22	Choose Wisely	85
Day 23	Enlist Enthusiasm	89
Day 24	Master Your Emotions	93
Day 25	Know Your Kryptonite	97
Day 26	Eat Your Spinach	101
Day 27	Know That Impossible Is Nothing	105
Day 28	Find Your Will To Win	109
Day 29	Be Content in Every Season	113
Day 30	Welcome the Struggle	117

CONGRATULATIONS   121
THERE'S MORE TO COME...   122

Foreword

When you think of your own success, what do you see? Do you see yourself in good health, financially wealthy, or running your own business? Maybe you visualize a promising career, a well adjusted family life, or the mere feeling of being happy and content. Regardless of what you envision, each of us has, or should, have some idea about our vision for success. A vision not created for us by the standards of society, but one that we have personally crafted and developed to represent where we want to be and what we desire to accomplish in this thing we call "life."

In the pages that follow, A'Yanna Webster illustrates that success IS possible for each of us, and gives us useful insight on how to take our "personal" vision of success to the next level. It takes someone with a vision of the possibilities to attain new levels of success, someone with the courage to live their dreams. And if you are going to achieve success on a new level, you will need to not only have the desire, but you will also need to possess the "know how." If you have the desire, A'Yanna will give you the know how through the readings in this book. So, buckle your seat belt and get ready to embark on a 30 day ride that will provide you with the tips, ideas, strategies, and techniques employed by some of the most successful people in the world.

It is a proven fact that those who are truly successful in achieving their dreams and goals share common characteristics. While these simple characteristics are not a secret and can be adapted by almost anyone who has the desire, they still tend to evade many people. A'Yanna, in *Winning Ways How to Achieve Success… No Mater What*, gives us a straightforward guide to adopting these characteristics, or ways, of those who are winners. She helps us to understand that if we are ready to move toward success, then it is time to take action and to make a change.

Now is the time to take on the *Winning Ways* that will bring about the necessary change to get you to your place of greatness in the **Winners' Circle**.

So let me, Les Brown "The Motivator", personally invite you to join me, and A'Yanna Webster, in the "***Winners Circle***". I know that after you complete this journey, you will be well on your way to achieving the success that awaits you. I challenge you to look for ways to be an active force in your life. Take charge of your destiny. Design a life of substance, and truly begin to live your dreams.

Les Brown
Motivational Speaker & Author

Introduction

I had often heard it said that if a person did something consistently for twenty-one days, whatever was done would become a habit. I thought I'd try it. Dragging myself to the gym for twenty-one days straight was rough, but I did it, and for a while, my routine did become a habit. But all too soon, my habit, well, was no more. After thinking about what I had done, I decided to take this "consistency concept" a bit further. What if I could do something consistently for more than twenty-one days? Let's say thirty days. What would happen then? Would it be easier to maintain the activity with more longevity? When I increased the number of days, I made this amazing discovery. What I found out revolutionized my life! This "something" that you do becomes more than a just a habit; it becomes a "way" of life. It develops into what I call a **Winning Way**.

This "way-of-life" concept is the focal point of *Winning Ways How to Achieve Success…No Matter What*. To further build on this concept, let's start with a basic definition of **Winning Ways** to help you to better understand the principal concept of this book. *Winning*, by definition means "arriving at a place or a state of success." *Way* is defined as *"a characteristic, regular, or habitual manner or mode of being, behaving, or happening."* Thus, **Winning Ways** are "essential characteristics for becoming successful; they are modes for arriving at your place of success." In other words, **Winning Ways** are basic to your success.

Now that you know what **Winning Ways** are, let's move on. In the next 30 days, you are going to develop the **Winning Ways** of thinking, walking, and talking like a success. As you develop these **Winning Ways**, you will gradually move from thinking, talking, and walking — to ultimately being. *Being* a success! It is one thing to walk the walk and talk the talk, but it is another thing to *BE*.

To *BE* successful at anything, much effort is required, and the decision to succeed is yours, and yours alone. The great playwright William Shakespeare raised an important question through one of his tragic heroes when he wrote, "*To be, or not to be – that is the question*" (*Hamlet*, 3.1.56).[1] This truly is the question that you will need to answer for yourself. To *BE* a success or not to *BE* a success? This, indeed, is the question. If your answer is "To *BE* a success," this means you now possess the first thing necessary to begin your success journey – *desire*. But desire without *know-how* is futile, and that's where this book comes in. *Winning Ways* provides the *know-how* to work alongside your desire to birth your success! So, if you truly have the desire, get ready to go with me on this **30-day success journey** – an adventure that is sure to make a difference in your life and put you on your path… To *BE*!

What can you expect in the next 30 days?

1. Expect to **BE CHALLENGED.** You will be challenged to think about, say, and do some things that may be unnerving, yet necessary in this process. But in this discomfort you will grow, so just think of it as growing pains. Commit to stretching yourself, and my promise to you is this: it will make a difference in your daily life and in your future.

2. Expect to **BE EMPOWERED.** *Empowerment* is about giving you the **T.I.P.S.** you need to succeed – in other words, the *tools, ideas, principles,* and *strategies* necessary to make your success happen. While it is one thing to be motivated, it is another to be empowered. Through empowerment you are given what you need to take

---

[1] George Lyman Kittredge, ed., The Kittredge-Players Edition of the Complete Works of William Shakespeare (New York: Grolier, Inc., 1936), p. 1167.

action in your life. And by taking action, you will continually move forward in your success journey. At the end of each **Winning Way**, there is a section called **Winning Application.** This portion of the book will empower you to apply the daily **Winning Way** to your life. In this manner, you are not just reading, but you are also taking action to apply the principles to your daily life.

3. Expect to **BE RENEWED.** If you have been complacent about your goals and dreams, now is the time to become *renewed*, re-energized for your success journey. Many of us already know what it takes to get where we want to go, but we lack the energy that keeps us going. We must be *reminded* every once in a while. Reminded that being successful takes hard work. Reminded that there will be some challenges along the way. Reminded that we must be persistent. But most of all, we must be reminded that success *IS* possible! These reminders are the things that *renew* us and give us the strength to continue on in the face of adversity. The next **30 days** will be a constant reminder, because as you read these reminders, sometimes even aloud, and as they resonate in your mind, you will be strengthened in your belief that your dreams and goals are possible. Once these reminders have become a part of your psyche, you will find the fresh renewal you need to take on your success journey with even more energy, vigor, and vitality.

4. Expect to **BE TRANSFORMED.** As your mind is elevated, and your thinking about your success is renewed, you can only expect that you yourself will be transformed. With a fresh outlook about your success, you will find yourself transformed into the kind of person who knows that there are

no limits as to what you can achieve. No longer will you be a conformist and just sit by and accept what comes your way. You will find yourself transformed into a person who believes that whatever you are seeking in life is possible. You will know in your mind and believe in your heart that nothing is impossible to you. And because of this belief, you will find yourself to be a more ambitious, productive, and positive individual.

Making the Most of Your 30-Day Journey

My goal for you is that you will BE and BECOME, in the next 30 days, all of the things previously mentioned. But to do this, you will need to make the absolute most of the days ahead. Here are some tips to help you make the most of your experience.

1. **Set a time to do your Readings.** Set a specific time each day to do your reading, and stick to that time for the next 30 days. This will cause you to be consistent, and you will be well on your way to establishing a characteristic that all successful people need—*discipline*.

2. **Make use of the Winning Applications.** DO NOT SKIP THESE! This is a time for you to process what you have read and then apply it to the situations you face. Don't cheat yourself by neglecting to look at where you are in this whole process.

3. **Use your Journal Pages.** Journaling is an excellent way to record your progress, thoughts, and feelings. Journal pages have been made available to you at the end of each chapter. Use them to record how and what you feel over the next

several weeks. In the days ahead, you will find your journaling to be a great outlet for you; it will become your confidant/e on your journey.

4. **Enlist the support of those you trust**. Let someone know that you are reading this book and give them permission to check on your progress, to see whether or not you are keeping up with your readings and activities. You may also consider getting a "reading buddy" so that both of you can read the book together.

5. **Speak "life" not "death."** Your life truly does follow your words. So as you begin your 30-day journey, resolve that you will speak positively about yourself, everyone, and everything around you. What goes into you over the next 30 days should be reflective of what comes out of you. That which comes out of you should be words of life. Speaking your success daily is key to this process.

No Matter What!

Please do not mistake me! Know that in the next 30 days, as in the days of most people's lives, you may feel like giving up. Something may happen to you that will cause you to think about quitting this journey. This is typical, especially when one is on the brink of success. The road gets rough, and, well, it just seems as if it would be easier to turn around and go back the way you've already come, than to persevere and keep moving forward through the trials and obstacles that come your way. It is at times like these that the *no matter what* part of this success formula must kick in.

Yes, this book, *Winning Ways*, is a guide to achieving success, but in no way am I saying that achieving success will be easy. In fact, I am saying right up front that it will be hard. So, before you even start on this journey, I need you to commit to taking on a *no-matter-what* attitude. *No matter what* means simply that—*no matter what*—whatever your "what" might be. We all have, or will have, some "what" that can keep us from success, if we allow it.

But we must resolve that when that "what" comes against us, we will stand strong. Today, maybe your "what" is sickness. Maybe it's finances or lack of confidence in yourself. Or maybe it's the past mistakes you've made in life. Whatever "it" is, you cannot afford to make your "what" the center of attention. Whenever you do this, your "what" *appears* to become bigger than your dreams and goals. Instead of concentrating on your "what," make your **Winning Ways** your focus. They are the tools you need to overcome your "what." When you put your focus here, you empower yourself to overpower your situation with **Winning Ways**—your attitude, thoughts, and beliefs. Decide now, that each day as you read this book, and every day hereafter, that you are going to become a *no-matter-what-person*—one who presses toward the mark for the prize that is destined for him or her—**NO MATTER WHAT!**

The Charge

Finally, my **charge** to you is this: take on the next 30 days as if they were the last 30 days of your life. The number 30 is representative of maturity, growth and new opportunities. Over the next 30 days, I challenge you to take the opportunity to grow and mature. As you grow and mature in your ideas about success, your attitude, and even your developmental steps, you will see new opportunities arise. So, if you are truly ready to go with me on this journey, I invite you not just *to go* with me, but also *to grow* with me into the success God has predestined for you. You were created to be prosperous. Now is the time, and this is the season for you to come into your own. I, for one, know and believe that you are ready to step into your rightful place on this earth, your place of success and destiny! So what are you waiting for? Get going, and I'll see you at the end of your journey...**NO MATTER WHAT!**

Winning Quote

If you don't know where you are going, you might wind up someplace else.

—**Yogi Berra,** *American Baseball Player*

Day-1

Begin with the End in Mind

On this, the first day of our thirty days to a mindset of success, we are going to *begin with the end in mind*. Do this: close your eyes and envision yourself at the end of your journey. "What is the *end?*" you ask. The end is the place where you want to be in this life. Begin to envision yourself as you desire to be, in the places you want to be, with the people you want with you, doing the things you desire to do, and possessing those things you desire to have. This is YOUR success. This is the place, that in the next thirty days, your mind will visit daily, and in the end, where your heart will take residence. As you begin your journey into the life and mind of success, know that in the next thirty days you will be challenged to examine and do some things that you may never have done in your life. As you read, ponder, and even execute the daily **Winning Applications**, you may become uncomfortable. Just know that neither the mind of success nor success itself will come without some level of discomfort. (We'll discuss this discomfort more in depth in the next several days.)

In the days ahead, as you read and things begin to happen in your life, and in the lives of others around you, I challenge you to reflect and meditate on YOUR *end*. As you focus on the end, instead of your current situation, you will know that your end will arrive in due season. Your maintaining focus will make it easier for you to stay motivated to take actions which will lead you toward your end. As you focus on your end, each day you will find it easier to pick up this book. You will be excited and energized to see what is in store for you as you continue your daily readings. You will be empowered to see, create, and take action toward achieving your END. So, this is it, your first day toward developing and keeping the mind of success. I will be with you all the way. Keep reading, and watch yourself evolve as thoughts about yourself and success are developed each day.

Remember to keep *your end* in front of you, because IT is the motivation for adapting a mindset that thinks, creates, and lives success. The more you develop your thinking about success, the closer you will come to it. So get ready to spend the next twenty-nine days working on *you* and your concept of success. It is said that what we focus on, we create. As you focus on your success for the next several weeks, get ready to create an ENDING that you, before today, could only imagine in your wildest of dreams. Stay focused, be consistent, and know there is *NO thing*, except you, that can stop you from achieving success…**NO MATTER WHAT!**

Winning Application

On this first day, answer the questions in today's reading about what **your** *end* looks like. Write the answers to these questions in your journal section, and refer to it often, as you go through the next several weeks.

Winning Ways Journal

Winning Quote

It takes great goals to lead us out of our everyday limits into accomplishing more than we ever thought we could or would.

— **Robert Cooper,** *Author & Life Coach*

Day-2

Go for the Goal

Now that you know what your end looks like, it is time to make a plan and set some goals for getting there. As simple as it may sound, many of us don't succeed because we fail to set goals for ourselves. Goals are important because they help us to focus on the road to success. When I was writing this book, I found that the only way that I would be successful in completing it was to set goals for writing. I sat down and began to map out when I wanted to finish, and what needed to be done in order to meet this goal. Once I had a road map of where I wanted to be, and a deadline for getting there, I found the road to finishing the book much easier. It was easier because I had broken my larger goal into smaller goals. Once I had achieved those, I celebrated them. Ultimately, I was able to reach my long-term goal of completing my book, and because of my planning and persistence, you are reading this book today! This is just one example of how setting goals leads to the achievement of success, but there are so many more that are equally important. Maybe you have a story or two about how setting a goal, and sticking to it, helped you to achieve something extraordinary.

As I mentioned earlier, *goal setting* is a simple principle, but it is an important one. Yet it is one that many of us fail to enact on the road to success. We have our end in mind, but we have no road map for getting there. Imagine trying to take a trip across the country without a road map. You know where you want to end up, but without some means of direction, you will never get there. The same principle may be applied to your reaching the end destined for you. The goals you set are the means to your end.

Yesterday, in day one, we talked about knowing your end, but what is more important than knowing your end is having a plan that will take you to your end. Today, I want you to focus your mind on the success that you envisioned in your reading on yesterday. Now, ask yourself these questions: What goals do I have along the way? What plans do I have that will help me to get there? One thing to remember is that, in order to get where we want to go, each one of us must have both short-term and long-term goals that are in line with our vision. Remember to set your goals accordingly, and as you reach each goal, celebrate your victory. Reward yourself for your achievement. Bask in how far you have come and how close you are to where you ultimately want to end. But don't stop there! After all the celebrating, rewarding, and basking, you then must do what most people fail to do. *Set another goal!* Sit down and assess where you are and what is still needed in order for you to continue toward your success. Do more than just set your goal mentally; write it down. When you do this, you hold yourself accountable to the goals you have set for yourself. Every time you repeat this process, you will find that you are drawing closer and closer to the ultimate place of success. Repeat the process: set more goals, short-term and long-term, reward yourself in the midst of progress, and set yet *another goal*. When you do this, you will find success to be inevitable…**NO MATTER WHAT!**

Winning Application

Based on what you have written as your *end* from the **Winning Way** for day one, write out both a three- and a six-month goal plan for the ACTIONS you will be taking in the months ahead to ensure that your success comes to fruition, and that you will reach your desired end.

Winning Ways Journal

Winning Quote

Never give in! Never give in! Never, never, never, never— in nothing great or small, large or petty. Never give in except to convictions of honor and good sense.

– **Sir. Winston Churchill,** *British Prime Minister Statesman*

Day-3

Never Give Up

For the past two days we have visited your ability to have both vision and goals for your life. Now that you are aware of the importance of each, you will need to hold on to the principles for achieving each, and vow that you won't quit—you won't give up—until you have reached them. We all know that giving up is so easy to do. Yes, for most of us, it is much easier to "throw in the towel" than it is to roll up our sleeves and stay in "the fight"—*the battle for success*! The reason we are tempted to *give up* is that achieving success is something that does not happen overnight. Even though most of us would prefer it to happen quickly. There will be challenging situations, people, and events along the way that will make giving up seem like a good option. But what you must do, like the many successful people before you, is come to the realization that challenge is part of the success journey. Once you have resigned yourself to facing challenges, you WON'T give up—come what may.

There are many examples of people who have faced difficult moments on their journeys to success, but they refused to give up. For instance, when Henry Ford was told that his Model T Ford would never make it, he could have closed up shop and gone home. Because he refused to listen to the doubters, he became the inventor of one of today's greatest resources, the automobile. Consider the next example—one that should encourage anyone with a dream. There was a young man who apparently had made himself satisfied being a piano player at a bar. When a patron asked him to sing along with his playing, he very adamantly announced to her that he could not sing. After, a great deal of coaxing and persuading by the audience, the young man began to play and sing in a voice that was crystal clear. You now know that young man as Nat King Cole.

Like Ford and Cole, on your road to success, there will surely be days when you'll feel like "calling it quits." **Yes**, it happens to the best of us. Maybe you've even been there already. It's days like this that make you feel that maybe your best is just not good enough, or you feel as if your many efforts are in vain. We all have come, or will come, to a day like this—a day riddled with so much doubt and fear about what lies ahead, that giving up seems a viable option. Yet, it is in these times that we must fight even harder to win the prize. Despite our emotional state, which, in fact, is very real to us, there is another reality within each of us, and that reality is the *will to win*! On the days when you feel like throwing in the towel, or sitting on the sidelines, remember that giving up will not make achieving success *any easier*. In fact, if you give up, it will make your goal that much harder to achieve. Instead of giving up, focus on your goal, knowing that as you persevere during the trying times, you will be victorious. If you will just keep striving, soon you will cross the finish line to success! And at that very moment, you will feel the pleasure of knowing that, even when the road was long and you were tired and weary, you stayed the course. Tell yourself today that you WILL hang in there, despite the circumstances. Don't you dare *give up*...**NO MATTER WHAT!**

Winning Application

Each of us needs a reason to press forward. Today, come up with three reasons why giving up *is not* an option. Of these three reasons, which one or ones stand out as being the one or ones for which you are most willing to stay the course? Whom or what do they involve? The next time you feel like giving up, refer to these three reasons as a reminder and a remedy for your staying in the race.

Winning Ways Journal

Winning Quote

Focus on competition has always been a formula for mediocrity.

— **Daniel Burrus**, *Author*

Day-4

Compete Against the Best...YOU

Now that you know that you cannot give up, today let's talk about not *giving in*. When most of us give in, many times it is because of the *perceived* competition that surrounds us. Let me explain. There are several factors that I give credit to for the many successes I have achieved in life. One of the most important factors has been my ability to put and to keep competition in its PROPER place. We have been taught from childhood through adulthood that the way to win or to be successful is to *beat* someone else, or "the competition." We are socialized to believe that winning is everything, and that if we do not win, then we lose. Yet, I have found this theory of competition to be untrue. You see, it is not the other person in the race that truly determines whether you win or lose. It is YOU! In your quest for success, YOU are the standard by which you should judge yourself.

Many times, we get so caught up with the abilities and accomplishments of others that we don't give ourselves credit for the many achievements and progress we have achieved in our own right. Whenever we belittle ourselves this way, we lose focus on our goals and our vision for our personal success; and we, in turn, put our attention on what others have been able to achieve. When I was a pageant contestant in the Miss America Pageant System, I won every single pageant I ever entered. "That's impossible!" you might say.

"But how?" Well, here's how. In each pageant, I was not competing "against" the other contestants. I was competing "with" the goals I had set for myself going into the competition. I was competing against my *history of achievements*. Having achieved my personal goal going in, I emerged a winner every time—many times even receiving the physical crown as well! When I knew I had done my personal best, even if I did not receive the top prize, I was then satisfied that I was a winner. Someone else may have won the crown, but I was *still* a winner, and *never* a loser!

When you put competition in its rightful place, you give yourself the power to be the only person in your race. Think about this: if you are running a race and continue to look across the lane at the next man, what do you think will happen? You are bound to be distracted. It is this type of distraction and attention focused on others that will cost you the win every time. Focusing on your competitors gives them an immediate advantage over you. Never allow yourself to be distracted! Instead, go out there and run your race as if you were the only person in the contest. Hold your head up high and keep YOUR focus on the finish line. My advice to you is this: set goals for your success and make every effort to achieve them. When you do this, you are already a winner! Know and believe that competing against the personal standards you set for yourself is the best competition there is...**NO MATTER WHAT!**

Winning Application

Today, answer the following questions in your journal: Whose standards am I competing against? What do I consider my competition? Against whom am I competing? Now think about an area in your life in which you are involved in competition—career, family, business, etc. Then ask yourself this question: Why am I competing in this area? Spend time answering the questions we have raised to get a better understanding of how you view competition. Then determine if your view is helping you or hindering you.

Winning Ways Journal

Winning Quote

There is no fate that plans men's lives. Whatever comes to us, good or bad, is usually the result of our own action or lack of action.

— **Herbert N. Casson**, Author

Day-5

Take Action

"**T**ake action right now! Take action right now!" I can hear the commanding voice of my friend, speaker, author, and coach, Kevin Bracy, as he encourages his audiences to repeat this mantra. It is a mantra that every winner must live by in order to attain success. Ask anyone who has ever achieved any significant feat in life how he or she did it, and you are sure to hear a similar answer: "I did not stand idly by, waiting for that 'big break.'" No, what you will find is that successful people *take action*!

When I think about the importance of taking action, I am reminded of a verse from the Bible that says, "Faith without works is dead."[1] Your works are your actions, and without them, your success is *dead*. You can *dream* BIG, *think* BIG, and even *plan* BIG; but if you never take any steps toward making your dreams, thoughts, and plans a reality, you will find that they are just that—dreams, thoughts, and plans.

Have you ever wondered why some people really seem to have a vision for their lives, but the vision never becomes a reality? For that matter, you may be such a person. You know that you have a vision for your life, and you are taking action, but things seem to be going nowhere. If you feel like this, ask yourself these questions: *Does my vision line up with what I know God wants for my life? Does my vision impact and empower the lives of others in some way?* If you answered

---

[1] James 2:17 KJV.

these questions in the negative, then reevaluate your vision, using the two questions above to guide you, and then TAKE ACTION!

When we take action, we put feet to our faith to walk in the promises of God. With every positive action we take, we move one step closer to the prize. With every negative action or lack of action, we separate ourselves and move farther away from our prize and our place of destiny. Yes, each of us has a place of destiny that we were created to reach. Yet none of us will reach that place without hard work, dedication, and ACTION. Think about where you are today; then think about your end, and the goals you set on yesterday. Now envision yourself there! Can you see it? Do you like what you see? Then you must TAKE ACTION TODAY! In the end, it is the action you take that will determine what and who you are to become. So, don't just sit there; get up and TAKE ACTION...**NO MATTER WHAT!**

Winning Application

On Day 2, you wrote down your goals and a plan for achieving those goals. What actions have you taken since that time toward setting your goals in motion and making something happen? Today, go back and review your journal entry and your plan. Make sure that your plan has action steps and deadlines attached to it. If it does not, take the time to jot them down as you create a realistic action plan that can be implemented within three to six months.

Winning Ways Journal

Winning Quote

Success is dependent upon the glands—sweat glands.

– **Zig Ziglar**, *Success Trainer, Author, Speaker*

Day-6

Hard Work Is the Key

We know from yesterday, that taking action is very important to one's success. But today, I want to share with you how *little action*, or *no action* at all, can literally "make or break you." Let me take you back to my childhood. I was eight or nine years old and working for my grandmother, who babysat relatives and other neighborhood kids. My job was to do, well, whatever my grandmother told me to, and at the end of the week she would pay me five dollars. It was an easy job. All I had to do was stick around and do a few chores here and there, and, voila! I'd get a nice crisp five-dollar bill at the end of the week to go to the store and spend on whatever I wanted. Sounds pretty simple, right? Well, wait until you hear the rest of my story, and you'll understand why I said that *hard work is the key*.

At the end of one particular week, I recall running in as always, after all the other kids had left on Friday, and holding my little hand out to receive my weekly pay. I'll never forget what happened next. My grandmother placed in my hand two one-dollar bills. I stood there waiting for her to put the other three in my hand, but she just stared back at me blankly. When I dared fix my mouth to ask her where my other three dollars were, this is what happened. In her very quiet, but very matter-of-fact manner, she reminded me that I had chosen to spend most of the work week outdoors playing kickball with the other kids in the neighborhood. She explained to me that, because I had chosen to put "little" effort into my work, my money was now just as "little." "Little effort," she said, "little reward." Although what she said makes sense now, at the time her words just didn't seem fair. Truly that day, I learned a very valuable lesson that has stuck with me until this day. What I learned was this: my reward is based on the amount of hard work that I put in.

As the years passed, the lesson my grandmother taught me took on an even greater meaning in my life. It taught me that you get out of life exactly what you put into it! If I wanted a great reward, what I wanted would require great work. On the other hand, if I wanted to do just enough to get by, that's exactly what I would be doing in life—just getting by.

Another important lesson I learned is that our success and rewards in life are directly linked to the amount of work that we *choose* to put into making whatever we desire happen. If you are willing to work hard at whatever you desire, eventually success will come. The key questions you must ask yourself are these: How much do I want out of life? How hard am I willing to work? The answers to these questions will be the determining factors in the actions you undertake and the rewards you receive.

The more you want in life, then without question, the harder you must work. This may mean that you will have to *break a sweat* as you pursue your goals. The process can be compared to working out at the gym or running along the track. The harder you work, the more you sweat. But this is good. The more you sweat, the greater the payoff in the end. You don't really mind the sweat; all you know is that you're expecting some results. In the end, you discover that the results were worth the effort. You look better, and you also feel better about yourself! Even though some of us may not like to sweat, it is one of the best measures of judging how hard we are really working. Success is determined by the glands—the *sweat glands*—and not necessarily by the family into which you were born is really true. No, your last name may not be Rockefeller, Trump, or Kennedy. Your name could be Johnson, Brown or Smith, or whatever, but what matters more than a name is the SWEAT glands. What matters is how hard you are willing to work to achieve the desired results. My friend, you are destined to reap the rewards of success when you learn that it is HARD work that determines the rewards you receive...**NO MATTER WHAT!**

Winning Application

Are you working hard daily at your goals, or are you doing just enough to get by? Yesterday, we talked about taking action, but today I am challenging you to take *meaningful* action. Today, step up your game and do whatever it takes to see some sweat. If you aren't *sweating*, chances are you aren't working hard enough. Your goal today is to evaluate the actions you are taking and then do something that moves you out of your comfort zone — something that causes you to *break a sweat*, something out of the box! Record this in your journal.

Winning Ways Journal

Winning Quote

Even when the urgent is good, the good can keep you from your best.

— **Helen Keller,** *Author/Lecturer*

Day-7

Prioritize Your Life

When I was younger, like most kids, I did not know how to *prioritize*. This is pretty obvious from the story I shared with you on yesterday. However, with time and wisdom, I have learned that to be successful, you must be able to manage time well. The most successful people I know have one thing in common—their ability to *prioritize*. In this fast-paced world in which we live, our time is extremely limited; therefore, time management is definitely a necessity. Work, family, church, business, clubs, and a number of other duties consume so much of our time. As a result, we oftentimes forget a very important aspect of our lives—*ourselves* and our personal goals and dreams. We take on more commitments, more people, and more responsibilities—things that keep us from working toward achieving our personal goals.

For some of us, keeping busy is a way to avoid taking action toward the things we really want to do with our lives. Some of us bury ourselves in menial tasks that bring us little joy or satisfaction. Others simply have not mastered the skill of saying *no*, even to people and things that may be important to us. Whatever the case, you must know that to achieve personal success, you must make *your* success a priority. Then you are free to prioritize the rest of your life.

I have a friend who once struggled in the area of prioritizing. Although she was very actively involved in many activities, she really was not "her best" at any of them.

She was often late to meetings and other functions, and when she was there on time, she had very little of herself to give. More than that, she continually talked about the things she WOULD do in her life and for herself IF she had time. My friend is a prime example of how we as humans allow ourselves to become so consumed by activities, things, and people, that we lose sight of what is most important. Sometimes we lose the energy even to pursue what means so much to us. My friend later realized that she was doing more and giving more of herself than she could afford to give, and she began to assess what was most important in her life. Today, she is happy, well-rounded, successful, but most importantly, sane!

You see, life is all about choices! What you choose to spend your time, efforts, and even your money on will ultimately determine how far you will go and what you receive out of life. So what will you choose? Because your personal success is so important, make the commitment to spend time each day working toward achieving it, in addition to the many other things you are doing with and for others. Decide that your success is a priority; then sit down and begin to evaluate what things in your life are helping, and what things are hindering your success. Make a commitment to use the time you have wisely. Remember that no one *ever* becomes a true success without making that success a priority. Choose never to allow the *good* to keep you from achieving your *best*...**NO MATTER WHAT!**

Winning Application

Do two things today. First, create a list of the *top-five most important things or people* in your life. Then next to each item, list how much time you spend in the course of a day focusing on that item. Do the numbers add up? Does how you spend your time reflect your numbered priorities? If not, then begin today setting aside time for those things or people that mean the most to you and your success. Then stick to that time! Make a timeline showing how much time you will spend on each priority in your life; then *take meaningful action.*

Winning Ways Journal

Winning Quote

When I create from the heart, nearly everything works, if from the head, almost nothing.

— **Marc Chagall**, *French Artist*

Day-8

Follow Your Heart's Desire

Yesterday, we spent time thinking about our priorities and their importance to us. I would be willing to bet that most readers listed *surface* priorities, those things that do not include their *true heart's desire*. Why would I draw this conclusion? The answer is simple. For many of us, our *desires* are not a priority, not even to us. But should they be? It is human nature to have desires—those things that we long, hope, and wish for, but many times go unspoken. Those things that you've been writing down as you've read this book—those things, no doubt, make up your *heart's desire*.

More than likely, most of your desires are locked up within you; they are the secrets that only your heart is privy to knowing and understanding. They are your forbidden fruit. Most times you try not to focus on them because they are almost taboo, because not even you believe that you can truly possess them. You can't share your desires with anyone; neither can you pursue them. Why? Because you might fail; then, everyone would know! Rather than risk failure, you re-channel your energy and focus on *all* the reasons why you cannot ever tap into the *passion* that lives within you day after day. You do what seems safe logically, and you create from the *head* and *not the heart*. Have you ever felt like this? If so, then you most likely are centered in fear, or you have allowed fear to overpower you. In essence, that which is binding you is the fear of what *is* and what *could be*.

Why is it that so many of us find ourselves victimized by fear? One of the reasons is that we have not been taught that having desires is all right. What we have been taught is that having desires is selfish, and even naughty. Webster defines *desire* as "to long or hope for; to express a wish for that which sometimes implies a general or transient longing, especially for the unattainable." But is there anything unattainable to those who believe? Absolutely nothing, for no good thing will be withheld from you if you believe.[2] This means that the thing you desire and think is unattainable can actually come to pass.

The desires you have for your success are matters of the heart. They have been put inside you to be lived out in faith, not in fear. Following your heart's desire, not your logical mind, is what will bring you the most success in life. Your success will come, not from your fears, but from your desires; not from your mind, but from your heart. You see, next to *know-how*, it is desire that will PUSH you to success. Your desire or passion will drive you when logic seems to fail. Desire will keep you pressing forward, even when your mind tells you to retreat. It will be your desire for that very cause, product, or idea you are passionate about that will bring you the greatest reward. However, before you can receive this reward, it is imperative that you reshape your mind to accept your desires and reject your fears.

Once you begin to follow the desires of your heart, you will be more empowered to do what it takes to ensure your success. Success trainer and motivational speaker Brian Tracy said, "The key to success is to focus our conscious mind on things we desire, not things we fear." The Scriptures tell us that God has not given us a spirit of fear, but He will give us the desires of our heart.[3] Today I challenge you to decide that you will not give way to your fears, but that you will embrace your passions and the desires of your heart...**NO MATTER**

---

[2] See Psalm 84:11c KJV.
[3] See 2 Timothy 1:7a and Psalm 37:4b KJV.

Winning Application

Today, you have another chance to really consider what you want out of life. What are your desires? List at least one desire you have—one that even you have thought to be unattainable until now. What has your mind told you about this desire that has stopped you from pursuing it? Today, your challenge is to examine this desire from the *heart* and not the *head*. When you use this approach, you put yourself on the right path to turning your desires into reality.

Winning Ways Journal

Winning Quote

Do the thing you fear to do and keep on doing it... that is the quickest and surest way ever yet discovered to conquer fear.

– **Dale Carnegie,** *Success Trainer*

Day-9

Recognize Your Fears

Yesterday, we looked at how your desires can become stifled by fear. Today, let's take a look at how *fear* can be a detriment to your overall success. Most times our greatest barrier to achieving success is FEAR. As foolish, or as contradictory, as it may sound, many of us are afraid of being successful. We fear the responsibility that comes with success. We fear what others will think. We fear that we will fail, so we do nothing. Whatever the case, I would be willing to bet that whatever your fear is rooted in is what stagnates you.

But what is F.E.A.R? I've heard it said that F.E.A.R is nothing more than *False Evidence Appearing Real*. It is those beliefs, circumstances, and sometimes people, that tell us that we cannot DO or BE those things that we know and believe we were called to do and be. Recently, as I was getting closer to finishing this book and starting on my first music CD, I began dreaming about plane crashes almost every night. At first I ignored them, chalking them up to an actual plane crash that had affected my life. But after the third night or so, I decided that there was more to the dreams, so I began to explore them, as I do all my dreams. What I discovered was that my dreams about the plane crashing had less to do with what happened during my waking hours, and more to do with my own subconscious *fear of failing*. The soaring plane was indicative of my success and where I was destined to go. The crashing plane represented the subconscious anxiety, doubt, and fear I had about being able to actually achieve my goals and finish the many projects I was working on.

My real fear was not of a plane crash; rather, my fear was of failure, or of not being successful. Once I realized the war that fear was waging against me, I began speaking to that fear and to my inner man. I began writing and speaking all the reasons why I would not, and could not, fail—in my personal projects, in my ministries, as a wife and daughter, and on my job. I reminded myself, as I shared with you yesterday, that God had not given me a spirit of fear, but of love and of a sound mind. And believe it or not, once I recognized and spoke to my own fear, I went to sleep that same night and slept better than I had slept in days. I had CONQUERED fear! I had put fear in its proper place—behind me.

Even as you move into your place of success, there will be times when you are so close to success that even you will be *afraid* of what is about to be birthed in your life. But the formula to overcoming your fear is to do exactly what I did. *Recognize* it, *speak* to it, and, then, *conquer* it. To *recognize* fear you must first search yourself. To *speak* to it, you must simply open your mouth in faith and declare your victory. And to *conquer* fear, you must do as we said in Day 3—*take action*! Instead of taking fear along with you on your journey to success, take the confession of faith and the belief that you can do and have anything that you set your mind to. Along the way, as you continually recognize and reconcile your fears, you will become better equipped to exercise your faith and your words to achieve success. Right now, ask yourself what is it about success that you are afraid of? Only by acknowledging and confronting your fears will you be able to make room for success in your life. For it is at the point when you confront your fears head on that you affirm that there is *NO thing* big enough or small enough to keep you from achieving your success...**NO MATTER WHAT!**

Winning Application

So, what are you afraid of? What fears are stopping you from moving forward in your success? Make a list of them in your journal and then use the *Fear Formula* (Recognize, Speak, Conquer) to address each of them. Decide today that you will continually address the fears that come up so that you will not allow yourself to be stagnated.

Winning Ways Journal

Winning Quote

Success is to be measured not so much by the position that one has reached in life as by the obstacles which one has overcome while trying to succeed.

— **Booker T. Washington,** *African American Educator*

Day-10

Overcome Obstacles

Now that you have learned how to deal with your fears about success, let's spend today talking about another factor that can cause many of us to retreat on the road to success—*obstacles*, those things in life that none of us can escape. I can think of many hindrances that I have faced from childhood until this very minute. Even as I write this book, I am faced with obstacles at home, in my business, and within my family. Likewise, I am sure that as you read this, you, too, can think of obstacles you've faced in the past, and maybe even some that you are facing today.

Whenever I think about obstacles, I like to think about how others have overcome the pain and suffering that life often brings. Because others overcame their obstacles, this lets me know that I also have the power to do the same. Recently, I saw the movie *Ray*, which is based on the life of the legendary Ray Charles. As I watched the movie, I began to think about how much Ray had to overcome to achieve the level of success that he reached at the time of his death. Ray Charles overcame poverty, the death of his brother, blindness, racism, and drug addiction…just to name a few.

Later, after the full impact of the movie had set in, I began to wonder what Ray's life would have been like had he not been forced to contend with those obstacles? His life certainly would have been very different. Why do I say this? The reason is clear. Had Ray Charles never learned to stand up against adversity, he would not have fought to learn to "see" and hear in a "seeing man's world" to become a successful musician and businessman. And had he not overcome blindness, he may not have known that he had the gumption, or whatever inner drive would be necessary, to stand up against the many other trials he would face thereafter. It is the obstacles—the hurdles, the obstructions, and the restraints that we face—that make us stronger and wiser. Once you have overcome one hurdle, rest assured that another will come, but you will be better prepared to deal with it because you went through the last one and were victorious. Even as you achieve the successes you are to have in life, you will discover that these victories will not come without adversities. There will be trials and tribulations along the way.

The most successful people are those who have a "story" to tell. They will tell you that they encountered struggle after struggle to get where they are today. You won't hear how they "gave up," but how they "stood up" in the face of adversity. I admire the tenacity and the stick-to-itiveness of those who have been determined enough to move beyond obstacles toward success. These people are shining examples of the resolve that says, "Come what may, we must fight until the very end." When obstacles come your way, remember that your success greatly depends on your ability be an *overcomer*. As you overcome the obstacles, you are achieving *mini-successes* that will prepare you along the way. Every time you overcome one obstacle, you are successful, and therefore, closer to your greater success. Know that these *mini-successes* are but an inkling of what is in store for you, and that you have a reward even greater than the obstacles before you. Whatever comes, believe and know that you can make it over, through, and around each and every obstacle. You are an *overcomer*! Face each obstacle with the confidence of a winner; don't give up and don't give in....**NO MATTER WHAT!**

Winning Application

What obstacles have you overcome in your life? What obstacles do you need to overcome today in order to move forward? Make a list of both to see what you've already achieved and what you need to achieve in order to move forward in life. Is there someone you know who has overcome great obstacles in life and has been able to achieve a measure of success despite the situation? Make it a point to ask that person how he or she overcame, and how life might have been different had he or she not pushed through the obstacles. From this exercise you will see firsthand that overcoming your obstacles is the only *real* choice you have if you are to be successful. Record this exercise in your journal.

Winning Ways Journal

Winning Quote

The secret of success is consistency of purpose.

— **Benjamin Disraeli,** *British Prime Minister*

Day-11

Become a Daily Success

Yesterday, I gave you a small dose of the concept of *mini-successes*. And in today's **Winning Way** I want to further explore the concept of *success day-by-day*. Let's start by talking about what *success* is and is not. Success is not just something you become; success is something that you are! Success is not just a destination; it is a journey, and to get through the journey, you must travel everyday toward your success.

Success is much like the old adage that says, "If it walks like a duck, and quacks like a duck, well, it's a duck." Achieving success can be viewed in this same way; so let's try looking at it from this viewpoint. *If it walks like success, talks like success, and thinks like success* – IT'S SUCCESS! How, you ask, can walking and talking as if you are successful make you successful? Well, here's how. Your success is an ongoing process. It happens everyday. When you strive toward being a success in your everyday life you are destined to be successful. As you travel along your success journey, and toward your destination, success happens.

Success is not just a place that you arrive at after a period of time. No, success is what each of us should strive to achieve everyday in order to reach our ultimate *place of success*. Unfortunately, you can't spend your day lying in bed and watching soap operas, then go to sleep at night, wake up the next morning, and – *voila*, you're a success! It just doesn't happen! Even though we all have heard the term "overnight success," I'd be willing to bet that even those who have achieved this "label" did something the day before, and the day before that one to achieve success status. Simply put, each of us must make success a mantra that we live by daily. There can be *NO* day that goes by when you are not thinking, "What can I do today to be successful?"

Being a success boils down to being good stewards over what we do everyday to achieve our ultimate success. This means that the same energy you put into being the next Donald Trump, you must also put into being a good husband. The same energy that you put into launching the next *O Magazine*, you must put into taking care of your children, family, and other household duties. When we practice being faithful over the little things and other responsibilities, success cannot evade us. Then, when we are entrusted with the bigger successes in life, we will know how to handle them.

We cannot continually fail in our daily pursuits and expect success to be just around the corner. It just won't happen like that. In our quest for success, each of must meet the *duck test* in the adage I mentioned earlier. We must *walk* like a success, *talk* like a success, *think* like a success, but most of all, we must BE a success on a daily basis -in the here and now. Chances are, if you are not successful at your daily responsibilities and with the people with whom you interact daily, your journey to success will be long and frustrating. Most definitely, your destination will be hard to reach. Today, you must decide that you will achieve success in everything you undertake—success with your kids, spouse, job, health, and so forth. The more successful you are in managing your life as it is today, the more disciplined you will be in reaching the ultimate success you wish to achieve in the future. Choose today to be a *daily success,* and watch yourself zoom ahead on your road to success…**NO MATTER WHAT!**

Winning Application

Where is your focus today? Are you so focused on the success down the road that you are failing in your day-to-day life? Consider three areas in your life in which you will practice success. It could be family, health, business, work, or ministry. Whatever it is, make a plan and the commitment to succeed daily in this area and to be faithful over these things. Write down the ACTIONS you will take each day that will help prepare you for future success.

Winning Ways Journal

Winning Quote

Some say that knowledge is power, but I believe that the use of knowledge is empowerment.

– **A'Yanna Webster**, *Author/Inspirational Speaker*

Day-12

Empower Yourself

For the next few days, we're going to focus on some of the ways you can start working on becoming the daily *success* we talked about yesterday. With that said, let's take a look at today's key word, *empowerment*. I love the word *empower*. It is such a small word, but it has such a big meaning. To be empowered means *to be given power or ability*. When I travel and speak on this power or ability, I refer to T.I.P.S. — the *tools, ideas, principles* and *strategies* necessary to put action to your goals. T.I.P.S. are the "stuff" that your success is made of. You see, none of us were born with all the knowledge necessary to be successful. In order to get where we want to go, we need to seek out the information and the people who can help us get there. To be truly successful, not only will you need the *will to succeed*, but you will also need the *know-how*.

I can recall going to many motivational seminars through the years, but I didn't leave all of them feeling empowered. Some of those seminars and speakers really motivated me. Early in the session, I was all fired up and excited about "going for my goals" and "being my best." But at the end of the day, that is just what I was—excited. Still I had little or no direction on how to make things happen. Then there were other seminars, however, in which the speakers focused, not only on how I felt but also on what I would do once I left the seminar. They made sure that when I left I had some tangible T.I.P.S. that could be applied to my life so that I would see some measure of change, improvement, or success. You know what? I DID! This is what being empowered is all about. It is seeking out the knowledge that you need to be a success. And even today — day after day — I still read, talk to others, attend seminars, listen to tapes, and engage in research to find ways to give power to my own abilities. For me empowerment is not an option; it is a *must*.

Answer this question for me: Has a millionaire ever walked up to you and said, "I want to tell you how I became rich"? Probably not. But if you empower yourself by asking such a person, I am sure that he or she would be willing to share some of the strategies that have worked. They will also share those things that have not worked for them. But the key is asking and seeking out information that can help you to reach your goals toward success. As you begin empowering yourself through tapes, books, seminars, and even other people, you will find that there is a wealth of knowledge out there. This will make your personal journey to success a much easier one. As you continue to seek empowerment, you will see that your goals toward success are closer than you think. Actually, the more you strive to know, the more you will grow. The more you grow, the closer you will be to fulfilling your goals and dreams. I've heard it said that *knowledge is power*, but I believe that the *use of that knowledge is the source of your empowerment*. So don't just acquire knowledge; rather, empower yourself by using that knowledge! Somewhere in your treasure of information, you will find exactly what you need to be successful...**NO MATTER WHAT!**

Winning Application

What are you doing now to empower yourself to reach your goals? What are some of the things you can do or people you can talk to for information? Once you have answered these questions, your next step is to actually go out and empower yourself and take action toward achieving you success.

Winning Ways
Journal

Winning Quote

Quality questions create a quality life. Successful people ask better questions, and as a result, they get better answers.

— **Anthony Robbins**, *Success Trainer*

Day-13

Ask Without Forgiveness

One way to *empower* oneself, as we talked about yesterday, is to ask questions. If this is true, then why is it that so many of us are afraid to ask questions? What is it about questioning another's understanding of something that seems to intimidate the most confident of people? Think about this for a second. If by asking questions we receive answers, and in receiving answers we receive understanding, then why is it that we seldom ask questions? Or we avoid asking questions altogether? I subscribe to the notion that it is not that we do not want answers or understanding. The real reason we are hesitant to ask questions is that we don't want others to know that we don't have the answers already! Such a prideful mindset is dangerous, and it is one that will ultimately determine how much or how little success one will achieve in life. Think about it. Do you suppose that most successful people you know arrived at their present state by pretending that they had all the answers already? I'd say not. These people used the **Winning Way** of asking questions, and doing so *without forgiveness*!

I remember how little I knew when I first started my coaching and consulting business. I did not know anyone around me who was doing such a thing, so do you know what I did? I logged onto the Internet and began searching for people who were involved in coaching and consulting, specifically, people who looked like me. After much research, I found a young lady named Antoinette Ayers, who was a personal coach and trainer, and had a very similar background to mine. But I didn't just stop there; I e-mailed her and explained to her what I was doing. I asked her some questions about her experiences, she responded, and we set up a conference call to talk. During the call I asked all my burning questions. I did not care how "elementary" I thought they might have sounded. I asked them anyway so that I could get an understanding about what it would take to be successful in this type of business. I left the call feeling empowered and ready to move forward in my business plan, and that's exactly what I did!

When we ask the right questions of the *right* people, we put ourselves ahead on the journey to success. As we seek to achieve success in our own lives, we must seek wise council from others who have "been there and done that." We must debunk the belief that if you ask questions about something, you lack understanding. After all, in all our getting, the one thing we must get IS an *understanding*.[4] Today, there may be questions that you have about where you are going and what it will take to get you there. My advice to you is to find someone who can give you — not just some answers — but the *right answers*. For that matter, find more than just one someone, for there is safety in a multitude of wise counselors.[5] Commit today, that from this point on, you will ask questions without hesitation and *without forgiveness*...**NO MATTER WHAT!**

---

[4] See Proverbs 4:7 and 24:6.
[5] See Proverbs 11:14.

Winning Application

Look around you. Is there someone in your life that you can ask questions? Have you taken the initiative to talk to that person? Commit today to finding one to two people who are, or have been where you are trying to go. Write down a list of questions to ask them about their journey to success. Make sure to journal your questions and their answers to use later as a resource.

Winning Ways Journal

Winning Quote

Your playing small doesn't serve this world... and as you let your light shine you unconsciously give others permission to do the same.

— **Nelson Mandela**, *South African President*

Day-14

Let Your Light Shine

Another way to practice self-empowerment in your journey to success is to know who you are, and to be confident and comfortable in that. Much of the "personal" success I have achieved can be attributed to my knowing and being myself. Despite what others think I am, or think I should be, I have spent my entire life striving to be one thing—ME! The stance I have taken has been a great challenge, because many times one's being self-actualized or self-aware often breeds the wrong perception from others. I know myself to be confident, but those with a skewed perception sometimes label me as cocky or conceited. Those who really KNOW me are often brought to laughter, when they hear others misjudge me with little or no evidence. In spite of what people may perceive me to be, still, I must allow the real me to come forth. I must *let my light shine.*

The stigma of being over-confident has followed me since I was five years old. But I must tell you that it has helped me, not hindered me. It has helped me to stay focused and humble, but most of all, the tendency of people to misjudge me has caused me to be that much more driven. You see, each of us could be ashamed of being who or what we are, but what good would that do? When we fall victim to what others perceive us as being, we water "seeds of insecurity" in ourselves and in others. Nelson Mandela put it best in his 1994 Inaugural Speech when he said, "Your playing small doesn't serve this world. We were made to make manifest the glory of God that is within us. It's not just in some of us; it is in all of us. As you allow your light to shine, you unconsciously give others permission to do the same." Each of us was created to be a *light* in this world, but if we are not careful, we will allow the opinions of others to become our darkness. Let me tell you this: everyone will NOT like you. Now that you have been informed, the best thing you can do for yourself, and for them, is to GET OVER IT! As long as you stay humble, and focused, and know that all talents, gifts, and abilities come from God — and ARE NOT of your own doing — IT'S OKAY! Just as God has given you clever inventions, witty ideas, and creative projects, and they have been successful, He will do the same for those around you.

It is true that success is not just for some of us; it is for all of us. Yet, only some of us will hit the mark, all because of the choices we make. As you make the daily choice to succeed, do so, knowing that you are an example to those around you. Refuse to be ashamed of being confident in yourself and in what you are achieving. *Let your light shine*, so that others can receive direction from it, follow it, and receive a similar reward. The more comfortable you are with being successful, the more success you will breed. So go ahead and hold your head up high and be confident in who you are, what you are accomplishing, and who you were created to be…**NO MATTER WHAT!**

Winning Application

In what situations or circumstances do you find it hard to *let your light shine*? Find two people today and share with them something good that has happened to you, or for you, during the week. Let them see your excitement about life. Let them observe you letting your light shine.

Winning Ways Journal

Winning Quote

If you wish to travel far and fast, travel light. Take off all your envies, jealousies, unforgiveness, selfishness, and fears.

— **Glenn Clark,** *Writer*

Day-15

Travel Light

In today's **Winning Way**, we shift our focus a bit to talk about some of the things that can stop us from getting to our "end," –that is, "heavy baggage." We must learn to *travel light*. Have you ever begun packing for a trip and realized that you were taking too much stuff? I have. There have been many occasions when I was preparing to make a journey and became frustrated. I knew that I was trying to pack more clothes than I needed. The more stuff I had, the heavier the load, and the heavier the load, well, the harder the bags would be to carry. In times like these I had to step back and reassess my packing skills. I had to decide which things I really needed, and those that I could leave behind in order to lighten my load. Even though it was sometimes hard to do, I'd begin, one by one, piece by piece, removing those things I didn't really need — eliminating the excess baggage that was weighing me down.

The packing scenario is an excellent metaphor for describing what many of us experience as we prepare to make the journey to success. We have our hearts and minds packed with a dream, goals, ambition, determination, and everything we'll need to make the success journey. We know exactly where we are going, and many of us even know the path we must travel to get there; yet, we cannot arrive at our destination because we are weighted down with excess baggage. In this case the excess baggage isn't those extra shoes or that extra suit you think you just can't leave behind. No, this baggage is the kind that, if carried, can weigh down even the strongest of people. Our excess baggage includes those un-affirming feelings, thoughts, attitudes, and beliefs that we carry within us, and they can keep us from arriving at our final destination. You know the ones I'm speaking of—unbelief, fear, envy, doubt, shame, and guilt, just to name a few. These are the things that weigh us down. This is the "excess baggage" that keeps us from making the success journey. When we try to move forward in life without addressing these negative feelings, most of us do not travel very far. If you do manage to make it down the success road with this type of negative baggage, you will find that it's just not that much fun once you're at the end. You'll find yourself living your dream, but you'll discover that your dream has turned into a nightmare.

We see many examples of shattered dreams when we look into the lives of some celebrities. Many seem to have everything that they could possibly want or need; yet, so many of them are still struggling with personal problems because of "baggage" that was not discarded on the road to stardom. There is an African proverb that says, "Where there is no enemy within, the enemy on the outside can do you no harm." Know today, that as you prepare for the journey of success, there is nothing that can stop you, or weigh you down, except that which comes from within you. When you choose to *travel light*, by identifying and addressing those things that will make your journey tedious, you make it easier on yourself to stay the course. You can then enjoy the benefits of reaching your destination. What excess baggage are you carrying today? Is it weighing you down to the point of frustration? Whatever your excess baggage may be, choose today to get rid of it. Once you do you will travel far and fast toward success…**NO MATTER WHAT!**

Winning Application

Take a close look at the *baggage* you are carrying today. How much of it is the "good stuff," and how much of it is the extra stuff that weighs you down? Identify your *extra baggage* now, and take action toward addressing each issue so that you can *travel light* on your road to success.

Winning Ways Journal

Winning Quote

Your past should be a place of reference, not a place of residence.

— Author Unknown

Day-16

Put the Past Behind You

In order for many of us to even begin traveling light, or traveling at all, we must learn how to *put the past behind us*. So today, we are going to focus on just that — not on the past, but on *putting the past behind us*. We know that the past has the power to shape the future, but it is how we view our past that determines whether that power is positive or negative. For ninety-nine percent of us, the past is a place where we look back and see all the things we *could* or *should* have done. Yet, when we truly look back on our lives, we will find decisions we made which both helped us and hindered us. Instead of focusing on those decisions that helped us, why is that so many of us focus on the latter? We are prone to play the blame game. We focus on who did what to us, who did not treat us right, who lied, who cheated, and on and on we go. When we focus on those things, we make them the center of our lives. We are saying that the things in our past are more important than the things in our future. In other words, we give our past the power to determine our future.

Let's use an athletic event to further explain the principle of keeping our focus in perspective. Let's say you're in a race and you want to get ahead. Where should you focus your attention? On what is ahead of you, of course. If you try to run a race looking backwards, there is no way you'll come even close to winning. Well, the same principle holds true in the race of life. If you live life constantly looking backwards, you'll never win. Instead of gaining ground, you will struggle to move forward. The life you have led thus far should not be the only life you will lead. That life should be just what it is—a *past* life. It becomes your responsibility to take the good from the past, and use it, take the bad and learn from it, and then, move on.

Because *the past should be a place of reference, not of residence*, we must, therefore, use the past as a gauge for making decisions with the intent of moving forward. When we unpack our bags, move in, and become comfortable with the past, we miss the opportunities that await us in our future. Instead of focusing so much on the past, we should concentrate more on the present, for our present truly is a great gift. The *here and now* is more precious than anything that has happened in your past. For the present is your NOW time, and what you do NOW is what will determine what you get out of your future. Whether you view your past as productive or non-productive, it is what you do today that will determine the success you will have in the future. Everyday we each have a new opportunity to put the past behind us, and work in the present toward our future. Despite where you have been and what you have or have not done, you have the chance to put old things behind you and press toward the mark.[6] Whatever that mark or prize is for you, know that the past can't stop you from getting where you want to go, but what you choose to do *today* can...**NO MATTER WHAT!**

---

[6] See Phil. 3:13, 14 KJV.

Winning Application

What situation, circumstance, or issue in your past do you keep looking back on? Whatever the problem, choose today to do these four things: (1) acknowledge it, (2) confess it, (3) learn from it, and (4) move on. Decide today to put that "thing" in its proper place—in the past.

Winning Ways Journal

Winning Quote

When life knocks you down, try to land on your back. Because if you can look up, you can get up.

— **Les Brown**, *Motivational Speaker/Author*

Day-17

Be Resilient

As we learn to put the past behind us, we are also developing another skill called *resilience*. As you put the past behind you, you must be able to rebound in order to move forward. You must be able to bounce back from whatever hand your past has dealt you. The way in which you bounce back will determine your fate in the end.

Have you ever stopped to think about how *resilient* children are? We can learn many lessons just by watching them as they face the challenge of growing up. The other day at a meeting, a cute blonde-headed boy dressed in overalls caught my attention as he experimented with what appeared to be a new skill. He looked to have been about two years old, and from all appearances, had just begun trying to learn to walk. I observed him as he pulled himself up by holding onto his mother's legs. He took a few steps, still holding on, and then looked back, as if he were having second thoughts about going further. After much hesitation, he decided to let go of his mother's legs. He took a few steps, and then — PLOP! His little bottom hit the floor. However, it was not the fall that grabbed my attention the most; it was what happened next that really made me take notice. The little boy laughed and laughed! Not only did he laugh, but he also crawled back to his mom and started the same process all over again. After watching his several attempts, it occurred to me that this baby had something that all of us need — *resilience*. A couple of plops did not prevent his repeating the process. Even though he kept falling, he kept getting back up. Never once did he lose hope and just sit there on the floor. NO, he tried over and over again. That baby's ability to be resilient meant that he would soon master an important childhood skill.

Resilience is the "ability to snap back or to spring back; it is the ability to return to one's initial state." This is a quality that we must develop. If we are to be successful in our quest to achieve our goals, we must be resilient in all our efforts. We must have the ability to bounce back! When we fall short of our goals, like the little boy, we must learn to laugh, pick ourselves up, and start over again. Think about this: What if that toddler had fallen, begun crying, and never tried to walk again? Had he given up, he would never learn to walk, and if he never learned to walk, he would never learn to run. He would never learn to stand on his own two feet, for that matter. The same principle applies to you and me, and others as well, on the success journey. If we give up during the setbacks, we'll never experience the comebacks in life. The old saying that everyone likes a comeback is really true. If we simply give up, we'll never reap the benefits of staying in the race and seeing what the finish line looks like. Instead of giving up after a setback and sitting on the sidelines, we must be like the toddler, who may fall many times, but will eventually be successful in learning to walk.

Today, you must decide to have the mindset of *resilience*. When you are resilient, you will find that success is inevitable. It is inevitable because you won't stop trying. In your trying, you will find that you may fail, but you will also find that failures are nothing more than opportunities for you to learn and grow. When you fall during your walk toward success, pick yourself up and get back on the journey...**NO MATTER WHAT!**

Winning Application

On what or whom have you given up when you faced difficult moments? Analyze your reasons for not trying again. Being resilient is something you must practice in order to stay on track toward your goals. Here is your simple task for today: when you feel like giving up, think about the baby in today's story. He kept on trying, and you must do the same in order to walk your personal road to success. Decide today that you will be *resilient* in everything you do.

Winning Ways Journal

Winning Quote

In order to do something you've never done, you have to become someone you've never been.

— **Les Brown**, *Motivational Speaker/Author*

Day-18

Become Someone You've Never Been

After yesterday, I am sure that you are fired up and ready to start working at becoming resilient. For some of us, developing this skill is going to be harder than for others. For some of us, becoming resilient won't be as easy because what we have always done when we faced difficult situations was to retreat. We failed to bounce back and try again. If you are tired of retreating, there is a solution for you. You can learn to bounce back. You can become resilient and do anything else you want to do by *becoming a new person.*

    I know that you're asking yourself how this can be done. Well, let me explain. What is it that you have always wanted to do or be in this life? Chances are, whatever your answer, this desire is a part of your overall vision for your personal success. Now think about this: What is it that has stopped you from achieving your desire in the past, and what is it that you need to do in order to achieve this in the future? Well, today I subscribe to you that, in order to do or become what you have always wanted to, you must become someone you have never been. What do I mean by this? Well, let me explain. Consider the loathsome caterpillar creeping along the ground. What keeps the caterpillar going is that he knows that he won't remain the same always. He knows that he will undergo change, and when the process is over, one day he will fly. In order for the caterpillar to fly, it must become a butterfly — *something that is has never been before.* However, once the transformation takes place, the once-caterpillar, now butterfly, is able to do things that it never thought possible. A similar change process can happen to you — not necessarily a physical change, but an emotional or spiritual change. Like the little caterpillar, you can become something or someone you have never been.

In order to *become someone you've never been*, today and everyday hereafter, you will have to approach life from a different perspective—with a new attitude. In some cases it may be that, instead of always playing it safe, you'll have to *take risks*. Or instead of sitting back and waiting for good things to come to you or happen for you, you'll have to roll up your sleeves, go to work, and *make things happen*. Now, I am not saying to change who you are, but what I am saying is that different situations call for different actions and reactions.

I am sure that, at some point, many of us have looked at who we are or what we've become, and have observed personal characteristics that, if given the chance, we would change. I'm speaking specifically about the things that can potentially hold us back. All of us have them. Maybe you're complacent; or more simply put, you're just a procrastinator. Or maybe you're on the other end of the spectrum, and you're too pushy and need to fall back a little. Whoever you are, and whatever the case may be, if you are to become the person you are striving to be, you must do things differently from the way you have done them in the past. This transformation simply means changing, not necessarily who you are, but changing how you think, what you do, and how you do it. Remember that the caterpillar is destined to be a butterfly. You, too, can be destined for success, but a change must occur from within.

Many of us think that we can do the same thing over and over the same way and achieve different results. Likewise, we think that we can act the same way over and over and get a different response. This just does not happen. Repeating the same habits over and over again will bring the same results—it's called insanity! Instead of following the path of needless repetition, we, too, must be like that little caterpillar, who gradually changes from within. If we are to be *someone we have never been*, our transformation must begin from within.

If it is our desire to be transformed on the outside, we must begin our transformation in our hearts and minds; this change will then affect our actions. First, we must believe in our hearts that a difference can be made. Then, we will begin to think differently, and finally, we will act accordingly. When this happens, we become a new person, because we are no longer stifled by those old thoughts and attitudes that still seek to shape us into who or what we can become. Instead, we have become this new person from the inside out, and it is this *person that we have never been* that will lead us to things and places that we've only dreamed of in the past...**NO MATTER WHAT!**

Winning Application

What new habits, thoughts, or actions, do you need to take on today in order to *become someone you've never been*? Record them in your journal. Then number them in order of importance to your success. Now, make the decision to start practicing and mastering them daily so that you can transform yourself into a success.

Winning Ways Journal

Winning Quote

Successful people are successful because they form the habits of doing those things that failures don't like to do.

— **Albert Gray**, *Writer*

Day-19

Do More

Today, as you start working on becoming the new you on your road to success, you must know that it will call for you to *do more*. By this, I am speaking about more than just taking action; I am speaking about taking the *right action* — the kind that others who do not reach their pinnacle of success are not willing to take. I've said already that on the road to success you'll need to turn your focus toward yourself, take action, and put competition in its proper place. Don't be surprised when you run into people who are trying to make the journey following a different plan.

On this road, there will be many people, yet only a select few will make it to the final destination. You might ask, "What happens to those who never make it to *Destination Success?*" Well, I can only imagine that they run out of "gas" along the way. Or they pulled over at a rest stop, and, well, they're still resting! Such people tend to change their minds according to the situation. For example, when they start down the road to success and see a sign that says, DETOUR AHEAD, something happens. Their first thought is to turn around, if that is an option, or to take the next exit. Still others will see the journey as being too long, and will decide to take a shortcut. But then there are others, most likely people like you, who will see the same detour and will react differently. Determination and wisdom will kick in, and you will stay the course to arrive at your place of destiny. You'll see that same detour ahead and your patience will rise up. You will persevere.

You see, those who have learned to wait know that there is a time for everything. They may be required to wait awhile, but they know that their time lies just ahead. And yes, they'll see the long road ahead, but their perseverance will perk up because they know that *Destination Success* is not by any means an easy trip. Because it is not easy, only a few select people will have the will to do what it takes to get there — the will to DO MORE.

You see, to reach your destination, you will have to be willing to do more than others are willing to do. You cannot be satisfied merely with the *status quo*. Motivational speaker Les Brown, said, "In order to have the things tomorrow that other people won't have, you have to be willing to do the things today that other people won't do." If you *do* what everyone else does, you will get *what* everyone else gets, and believe me, everyone does not reach the pinnacle of success. But when you make the commitment to "go the extra mile" and to "stay the course," you put yourself in the position to arrive at your destination in record time. Today, you must decree: "I am willing to go the extra mile in order to reach my destination of success." Don't just say it; do it, live it, and become it, for it is the extra mile that leads you to the place that reads, NEXT EXIT SUCCESS! So stay the course, and do more, and more, and more...**NO MATTER WHAT!**

Winning Application

Think carefully about this question: What MORE can you do to reach your destination of success? In what area(s) do you need to become more focused? For each area, write down three or more ways in which you plan to achieve *more*. Then set a timeline for accomplishing each task on a daily basis.

Winning Ways Journal

Winning Quote

Give without remembering, and get without forgetting.

– **Willie Jolley**, Speaker/Author

Day-20

Give More Than You Get

As you start doing more, as we discussed yesterday, you will be in a better position in life to *give more*. In today's **Winning Way,** we look at the *gift of giving*. Yes, giving is a gift. Some of us have a natural ability to be generous. We have the uncanny ability to see and respond to the needs of others. Such people have what I call a "ministry for giving." They give without expectation, without regret, and without reward. These people give out of a genuine desire to help others in some way. Whether it is time, money, or talent, they give because giving is not only what they do; it is who they are.

Each of us has the ability to give something, not only to others, but also to this world in general. It is in our giving that we are made successful. I believe that if each of us is to become great in our own right, we must give our way to greatness. While it may sound contrary to what you may believe or have been taught, it is in your giving that you are truly blessed. Although many of us have been duped into believing that the way to get ahead is to hold on to everything we have, and to put our needs before those of others, this simply is not true. In fact, the very opposite is true.

When you choose to give to others, several things happen. First, you set in motion the principle of reaping and sowing. When you give, your giving ultimately comes back to you. Secondly, giving demonstrates your ability to show care and concern for others. And finally, your giving shows that you can be trusted with whatever time, money, talent, or whatever else you have. Let me explain this concept a bit further. If you are miserly in your current state, then it is fairly certain that with abundance you would be even more miserly. So the question is this: Would it be profitable to give more to someone who cannot be faithful in sharing what they already have? Along these same lines, if you are so caught up with hanging on to what you have, chances are when something better comes along, you'll "miss the boat" because all your energy will be focused on what you already have.

Maybe you are asking yourself, "What is it that I have to give?" The answer is very simple—you. As you give of your time, talents, money, ideas, ministry, and other gifts, you set yourself up to be successful. "How is this?" you ask. Well, I'm glad you asked. You see, nothing in life is free, including success. You cannot buy success, but you can put yourself in a position whereby success comes to you because of what you do for others and what you contribute to this earth.

When I think of this **Winning Way,** *giving more than you get*, I am reminded of Dr. Martin Luther King, who gave his way to greatness, by using his talent of articulation to speak for the rights of African Americans. He gave of his time, talent, money, family, and ultimately, gave his life. Because of his contributions, today he is one of the greatest men in history. Decide today that you will give more than you get. *Give without remembering*, but when you receive, get without forgetting. Your personal success is directly linked to what you sow into the lives of others, so start sowing today, not just for your success but also for the success of others...**NO MATTER WHAT!**

Winning Application

The concept that it is more blessed to give than it is to receive may be hard to grasp. Nevertheless, it is very true.[7] Take a moment to think about how you give to those around you. Are you giving enough of your time, talent, love, money, etc. to those who need it most? Decide which area in your life that you can give more, and make a conscious effort and plan to give above and beyond in this area. Today, find someone to whom you can give something, without expecting *anything* in return. As you do this continually, you will see yourself and others blessed through your giving.

Winning Ways Journal

---

[7] See Acts 20:35 KJV.

Winning Quote

Few people are successful unless a lot of other people want them to be.

— **Charles Browder,** Writer

Day-21

Build a Support System

As you continue to think about giving more, what better people can you give to than those who are there for you on a daily basis? These are the people whom I refer to as *your support system*. In your quest for success, it will be highly important that you have some good people surrounding you and encouraging you. I, for one, feel privileged to say that every measure of success I have achieved in life has been with the help of a support team. While there have been many players in my life, my most significant supporters have been my mother and my husband. In my quest to be and do many things, these two have been in my corner 110 percent of the way.

I have often wondered how successful I would be if I did not have a support system pulling for me. Many experiences I have encountered have taught me just how important a support system can be. Once I was preparing for a certification training in which I would be making a presentation for a national company. I received the two fifteen-page, forty five-minute scripts two weeks prior to the training certification, just before Christmas vacation. Although I had planned to spend my vacation resting, entertaining, and setting goals for the New Year, I found myself consumed with trying to learn the materials for training.

The first week of preparation went well. I got up each morning and started my learning process, and would repeat my studies in the evening. But by the end of week two, I was so frustrated and exhausted. Frankly speaking, I was tired of reciting and regurgitating the material. With only a few days remaining, and lots of material to learn, I did not "see" how I could be successful at retaining the rest of the material prior to my certification trip. My brain was on information overload! But in my time of frustration, it was my husband who gave me the support and strength I needed to keep going. "Baby, I know you can do this!" he reminded me constantly. He was the one who continually encouraged me not to give up. You see, even when I felt hopeless, my husband possessed enough *faith* in me to believe that I could still be successful. And he was right! I boarded that plane and went to the training, knowing that someone believed in me. Not only did I certify, but I also certified with the veteran speakers—a feat that had never been accomplished before. I had succeeded, not on my will alone, but with the support and love of those around me.

As you strive for success in your life, make it a point to surround yourself with people who believe in you, your dreams, and your goals. They are the ones who will be there with you during every season—in both drought and harvest. Because they know you, and know what you are capable of achieving, they will hold your feet to the fire. They will direct you and give you sound advice. Sometimes they may even correct you—but who doesn't need correction sometimes? To stay on the road to success, you will need to have people who support your efforts. You need passengers who know where you are headed. You will need those few people that you can count on to be there at both the start and the finish line. Now take a look around you to see who's on your team, because we all need good teammates—our *strong support system*—on the road to success...**NO MATTER WHAT!**

Winning Application

If you have not done so already, identify your supporters and share your personal success goals with them. Seek their support, guidance, and accountability in achieving your goals. Make the commitment to stay connected to your *support system* as you strive to see your success come to fruition.

Winning Ways Journal

Winning Quote

Some people you spend an evening with; others you invest an evening with.

— Author Unknown

Day-22

Choose Wisely

Today, we will begin where we left off yesterday. While it is important that we build a support system, it is even more important WHOM we *choose* to be a part of that network. In our effort to possess the "mindset of success," we must be mindful of those around us. In a little poem by an unknown writer, the following line appears: "Tell me who your friends are and I will tell you who you are." So, tell me. Who are the people with whom you spend your time? What are they like, and what value do they add to your aspirations and goals? The answers to these questions are vital to your success.

If you were to ask me the same questions I posed to you, I would be the first to tell you that from the time I was a young child even until now, I have not had many friends, but those I do have are an asset to my life. Even today, when I look at my own friendship circle, I find that those whom I call "friend" are those with whom I share my deepest thoughts, dreams, and ambitions. Likewise, they feel comfortable doing the same with me. When I think about it, there are very few people that fit this description; in fact, I can count them on one hand. You see, everyone does not deserve a front-row seat in your life. There are some who will take a back seat, being there for you, having your back, but never really having the inside view of where you are headed. Why? The reason is simple; they have a limited view of your overall plan for your life, and they just don't understand where you are trying to go. Then there are the "hitchhikers." They mean well, but honestly, they are just along for the ride. The hitchhikers are waiting for you to get to your destination so they can say that they were with you all the way. But those who have a front-row seat in your life will be there for you through every situation, during the good times and the bad times. No matter what is going on, they are still there in position—the front seat. This is what *choosing wisely* is all about. It's not about being *selective*; it is about being *protective* of who you are and where you are going. You should be so protective that you will allow only those special people to see into where you are going.

It is my hope for you that when you look at your circle of friends, you will find people who are ambitious, positive, supportive, and poised for success themselves. If by chance you do not find this to be the case, then you have a simple decision to make. You must decide that your circle of influence will be one that propels you to greatness. You must align yourself with those who have similar attitudes, values, and goals in life. It has been said that when two people go for a walk, one of two things will happen. *One will walk faster to keep up*, or *the other will walk slower so as not to leave the other behind*. The bottom line is this: one person's pace will ultimately have an effect on the other's pace. Today, you must declare that those who walk with you on the road to success will be those that help you to keep pace so that you will not fall behind. They will be there with you at the end of the race, for they, too, will have a goal to pursue and a victory to achieve. *Choose your circle wisely*, and you will experience success all around you...**NO MATTER WHAT!**

Winning Application

In your journal, make a list of your friends. What does each of them bring to your life? What do you add to theirs? The answers to these questions will serve as the basis for each relationship. Determine today whether or not you are *choosing wisely*. If not, make the commitment to do so, starting today.

Winning Ways Journal

Winning Quote

Success is not the result of spontaneous combustion; you must set yourself on fire first.

— **Reggie Leech**, *Canadian Hockey Player*

Day-23

Enlist Enthusiasm

As you begin thinking about the concept of building a support system and choosing wisely, I challenge you to think about the characteristics you possess. Consider the attitudes of the people around you. Then consider the characteristics of people who are winners. This will help you determine who, in your life, will make great teammates or fans in the "game" of success. One characteristic that you definitely should have yourself, and look for in others, is *enthusiasm*. If you plan to win in life, you will need enthusiasm. Why is enthusiasm important? We see the answer to this question in everyday events around us. For example, attend any given sporting event, and you will see that the winning team always has the most enthusiastic fans. Simply put, everyone likes a winner, and everyone likes to win.

In our **Winning Way** for today, we find that to be successful, or *to win*, we must enlist enthusiasm for winning. In order to help you fully understand this concept, it is necessary for me to ask you a question. What comes first, the *enthusiasm* or the *win*? Are the fans from the winning team enthusiastic because they are winning, or were they already enthusiastic when they arrived at the game? Good question. And let's not forget about the fans from the "losing" team. Were they enthusiastic when the game started, and then lost their enthusiasm as their team began falling behind in the game? I'd venture to say that both set of fans started out with enthusiasm, but somewhere along the way, one lost its tenacity. And once the tenacity was gone, they lost the belief that they could actually win the game. They looked at the scoreboard and calculated in their minds, that there was "no way" they could possibly come back and win. They looked at the success of the opposing team and reckoned, "Maybe they're just a better team." The more they looked at the scoreboard, the less confidence they had in their team's ability to take home a win. If only they could have "bottled" the enthusiasm they had when they entered the game, no doubt the outcome would have been different. When their team started to fall behind, they would have opened up that "bottle of enthusiasm," taken a big gulp and kept right on cheering. What an effect this would have had on that team on the field! Even while the other team was scoring, the opposing team's fans would still have been cheering their team on to victory. What a difference this might have made!

You see, the more enthusiastic you become about winning, despite what the game looks like, the better your chance of being victorious. You must begin and end each day with the same enthusiasm. Search for things and people to help you *enlist enthusiasm*. You simply can't afford to be without it. If you lack enthusiasm, you lack motivation, vision, and will. Even when others around you fail, you must make the decision to be your biggest fan. You must cheer yourself on whether or not you're scoring or waiting on the sidelines, when you make a huge play or even when you fumble.

If you are to be your greatest fan, you can't be fair-weather or "sometimey" in your will to succeed. You must understand that success will come, only if you continue to play hard and fair, and stay excited about the future that you know ultimately awaits you. You must stay in the game, and you will win, if you remain enthusiastic. Dr. Phil says it best in the sound bite from his opening credits, "I want you to get excited about your life."[8] Well, today, and everyday thereafter, that is exactly what I want you to do. Become excited, get "pumped up" — *enlist enthusiasm* — and get ready to cheer yourself across the finish line to success...**NO MATTER WHAT!**

Winning Application

What excites you about your life? What CAN you get *excited* about? Today, think about this question and journal those things that excite you. The next time you feel as if you are losing in the game, go back to what excites you and become your *number one cheerleader*!

Winning Ways
Journal

---

[1] "Dr. Phil", KCWE-29, Time Warner Cable

Winning Quote

If I feel uncertain I will raise my voice. If I feel poverty I will think of wealth to come. If I feel incompetent I will think of past success...today I will be the master of my emotions.

– **Og Mandino**, *Motivational Speaker*

Day-24

Master Your Emotions

Yesterday, we talked about the emotion of enthusiasm as a must-have trait in our effort to be successful. While it is important that we adopt certain behaviors and emotions, it is just as important that we rid ourselves of others. Balancing the two is called learning to *master your emotions*. In today's **Winning Way**, we look at how mastering your emotions can either make or break you on your journey to success.

Many researchers have believed over the years that it is the intelligence quotient (IQ) that determines whether or not one will be successful. But in recent years, others have begun to theorize that something more than intelligence is needed for a person to achieve success. Additional research in this area has focused on the role of the emotions as they relate to an individual's success. In other words, researchers are taking a look at the emotional quotient (EQ) along with the IQ. Many believe that emotional management is essential to one's success.

Right now, even if you do not believe yourself to be the most intelligent person on the face of the earth, you may possess a skill that can take you much farther in life than "smarts." It's called your emotional quotient (EQ). There are many unsuccessful people with high IQs, but they lack a good EQ. If we stop to think about it for a moment, all of us have known someone whom we've looked at and thought, "He or she has so much potential." For some reason, however, that person seemed not to have been able to utilize the potential that lay within. Maybe he or she had received all A's in school, and you barely squeezed by with C's. Yet that person just couldn't seem to grab hold of the success that would seem to be inevitable for someone so smart. The problem may have been that he or she lacked a good emotional quotient.

I subscribe to the belief that no matter how much intelligence or ability a person has, that individual cannot be successful if he or she is a slave to emotions. Such an individual has what is called a low emotional quotient. At the slightest sign of trouble, people with a low EQ often resort to hiding, running, or quitting. Intellectually, they are sound, but emotionally they are weak. On the road to success, when things *get rough*, the emotionally weak *get going*. They were born with intelligence and the ability to calculate complex problems, but they never learned or mastered the skill of *emotional management.*

Life is somewhat like being in a boxing match, which calls for a range of emotions. It really doesn't matter how smart you are, if you can't stay in the fight because of the external pressures around you. With a low EQ, you will not be victorious. But let's say you are of average intelligence, but you are a true fighter — one who "rolls with the punches" of life. When life knocks you down, you don't just lie there, you look up, and eventually, you get up. Remember, if you can look up, you can get up. The ability to look up is characteristic of a high EQ. The one who can get up is the one who will be standing when the last bell rings. No matter the level of your intelligence, when you allow your emotions to control you, you give in on ability and give way to fear, regret, doubt, laziness, and the other emotions that come with the day-to-day struggles of life.

I believe that the people who are most successful are those who remain so focused on their goals that they refuse to waiver in the midst of the bumps and bruises along the way. You see, no matter how smart you are, or how much talent and ability you may have; if you are easily discouraged and distracted, you can't stay focused long enough to achieve any measure of long-term success. Before long you begin retreating from the ring of success. Ask yourself, "What is my emotional EQ? Am I consistent in my belief that I can be successful, or am I allowing my emotions to toss me to and fro on my journey to success?" Whatever your answer, know today that to be successful, you **must** *master your emotions.* Lay aside every weight and decide that you will not allow negative emotions to determine what you do, who you are, or what you are destined to become. Know that what you feel is just that—a *feeling*—and if you will continue to stay in the fight for success, you will find yourself in the middle of the ring with your boxing gloves lifted high above your head...**NO MATTER WHAT!**

Winning Application

Are you being defeated by your emotions? Do you pursue your success only when you feel good? If so, you may have a low EQ. To determine if your EQ is having an effect on your success, for the next three days, journal what actions you take toward your goals and try to assess how you feel. Check to see if there is a direct correlation between what you did and how you felt that day. Also look at what is going on in your life. If needed, make a journal plan to improve your EQ.

Winning Ways Journal

Winning Quote

Our strength grows out of our weakness.

– **Ralph Waldo Emerson,** *American Essayist and Poet*

Day-25

Know Your Kryptonite

On yesterday, we talked about the importance of mastering our emotions. One surefire way to do this is to begin assessing both our strengths and our weaknesses. In today's reading we will focus on the importance of knowing our weaknesses as they relate to our success. We all love superheroes because they're strong and always see to it that good conquers evil. We call to mind Batman, Superman, Spiderman, and we can't forget the "sheroes" or super heroines like "Wonder Woman." While all of these characters are fascinating, strong, and courageous in their own right, they all have something else in common. You may have guessed already what that one thing is from the title of today's **Winning Way**. Their common thread is that they each have a *weakness*.

From our list of superheroes, let's take for an example, Superman. We all know that Superman's weakness is Kryptonite. Whenever Superman comes anywhere near this element, his powers and abilities become useless, and he becomes just like any ordinary man. He is unable to fly, to soar through the clouds over tall buildings, to burst through steel doors to rescue damsels in distress, or to save the world, for that matter. Kryptonite is the only thing that can stop Superman from fulfilling his purpose of being a superhero. What is important is Superman's awareness of this weakness, and it is this awareness that renders him successful in his heroic attempts.

Much like Superman's alter ego, Clark Kent, we too are everyday heroes. We have the power to make great change, positively affect others, and be successful in fulfilling our life's purpose. Yet, each of us has some form of Kryptonite that can potentially stop us from achieving success. Kryptonite is nothing more than that thing that makes one weak, or reveals one's weaknesses. Each of us has some Kryptonite — something that can stop us from reaching our goals. Maybe your weakness is complacency; you find yourself satisfied with mediocrity and can't move ahead. Maybe you're not a "people person," and your job requires that you be able to interact with a variety of people. Or, maybe you, like a number of others, allow your resistance to change to cripple you. Whatever your weakness is, in order to remain strong, you must *know your weaknesses and also what makes you weak.*

During most job interviews, employers will ask the question, "What are your strengths, and what are your weaknesses?" Many people can rattle on and on about their strengths, but they become stuck when it comes to talking about their weaknesses. But I believe it takes a stronger interview candidate to be able to talk about his or her weaknesses. An interviewee who acknowledges weaknesses has already placed himself or herself in a position of power to overcome those weaknesses. It doesn't matter how many strengths you have; if you do not know your weakness, more than likely, your weaknesses will overtake your strengths. If you do not know your weaknesses, you have no way of fighting against them or improving upon yourself.

Believe it or not, there is power in weakness! What I mean by this is that knowing your *weaknesses* makes you stronger. Most employers will tell you that they would take the person who knows his or her weaknesses any day over the one who has no clue as to the areas where he or she needs to improve. If you are to become successful, you must know the external forces that weaken you, as well as the internal, or personal weaknesses, that hinder you. In knowing this, you give yourself the power and ability to fight against them, and to eventually overcome them.

Today, despite your weakness or weaknesses, whether real or perceived, know that you are a *superhero*! You were created to go far beyond what man's natural ability can produce, and you will...**NO MATTER WHAT**!

Winning Application

What are your personal weaknesses? What areas in your life can you improve to help you move toward success? Identify at least three areas in which you can improve, and make the commitment to do so, starting today.

Winning Ways Journal

Winning Quote

I was always looking outside myself for strength and confidence but it comes from within. It is there all the time.

— **Anna Freud**, *Psychologist/Author*

Day-26

Eat Your Spinach

Just as we must know our Krypotonite, we must also *eat our spinach*. In the old cartoon, "Popeye, the Sailor Man," it was spinach that turned Popeye from just an "average guy" to a strong and courageous man. I can recall watching both the cartoon and the movie as a kid, and just waiting for the moment when Popeye would grab hold of a can of spinach whenever there was a crisis. There was something exciting in knowing that, with each adversity he met, Popeye could overcome it just by eating a little can of something I hated to eat—*spinach*! Once Popeye had his hand on that can of spinach, I knew that things were going to turn around for him, and fast, for in that can of spinach, Popeye found his strength. And just like our old friend Popeye, we too must find that *one thing* that strengthens us, and we must consume it—we must *eat our spinach*!

If you are to become successful, you must know what your strengths are—your natural strengths as well as your spiritual strength. You must identify the strengths you have and also those things that give you strength. If you are like most people, you do have weaknesses, and you must identify those weaknesses so that you can begin to fight them with your strengths. So then, what is that special something that gives you the power and ability to stay in the fight when difficulties arise? What is *your spinach*? You must know what it is so that you can rely upon it when you face times of need. For me, my sources of strength are the Word of God and prayer. They are what give me the strength and ability to continue my daily journey. I partake of both daily, feeding and building myself up. They are *my spinach*. For others it may be meditation, exercising, or reading. However, no matter what your spinach is, in times of need, hopelessness, and doubt, you must run to it daily so that you can become rejuvenated and reenergized for the journey ahead. You, too, will need to find your *spinach* in order to be successful in life.

The things that motivate and empower us will ultimately cause us to be victorious in all things. This **Winning Way** is one that not even the toughest of men can be successful without. Take for instance, the big, rough, and tough guys in the "Strongest Men Alive" contest. Even they could not be successful without tapping into their strengths, both mental and physical. They may use protein, do lots of bodybuilding exercises, and have the mindset that "I can lift this 1000 pounds, even if it kills me." But believe me, if those men did not strengthen themselves for the competition, they would not be able to lift nearly as many pounds. You, too, will need strength on a daily basis, because you will find that each day is "strong-man" competition toward achieving your success.

The stronger you are, the more weight you can carry, the more trials you can handle, the more circumstances you will overcome. The stronger you are, the less likely you will be to throw in the towel when negative forces come against you, and life seems too heavy a burden to bear. Today, I challenge you to find out what gives you the strength to carry on daily. Stock up on it as if this were your last chance, and in those times when you feel yourself becoming weak, don't forget to *eat your spinach*…**NO MATTER WHAT!**

Winning Application

What is it that gives you strength? When you feel weak, how do you handle the feeling? Today, I challenge you to find that one thing that you can run to when you feel like running away. Whatever that thing is, whenever you feel like giving up, go to it as if your life depended on it—because it really does!

Winning Ways Journal

Winning Quote

The only place where your dream becomes impossible is in your own thinking.

— **Robert Schuller**, *Author*

Day-27

Know That Impossible Is Nothing

Now that you have examined both your strengths and your weaknesses, it is time to accept them, change them, if necessary, and move forward in your walk toward success. Equipped with this good information about yourself, there is no limit to what you can do, unless you yourself set the limit. On this note, our **Winning Way** today focuses on taking the limits off our lives, and we can do this because we *know that impossible is nothing.*

What are limits? Limits are nothing more than mental barriers we create. These barriers block our progress and keep us from the finish line. We say that we *would* go back to school, but we are too old. Or we *would* start that new business, but we don't have enough experience. We *would* and *could* do a lot of things if we *would* only allow our mind-sight, or spiritual insight, to overcome what we see in the natural. When we use our natural vision, much of what we *would* do becomes nothing more than a thought, because what we see appears to be bigger than what we believe we can handle. Not only does it seem bigger than what we can handle, but it is simply more than we think we want to tackle. So we close our natural eyes tightly and hope that the vision we have for ourselves will just go away. We don't realize that the thing we perceive as impossible is really *nothing*.

Yet, when we look at the same difficult tasks with our spiritual eyes, what we see is totally different. Through our spiritual eyes, we have the ability to see ourselves doing and becoming exceedingly above that which we could ever ask or think. Through spiritual eyes we can see joy, patience, love, longsuffering, peace, and the other fruit we will need to be successful on this earth. Through our spiritual eyes, what seemed impossible now seems *doable*, and what seems doable, becomes *done*.

When you use your spiritual eyes, you see in you what God sees in you. You see that, with His help, all things on this earth are made available to you. Understand that you alone can do nothing in and of yourself. It is the God in you that gives you the ability to do and become those things that He has called you to do and to be. Understanding and believing this, then you know that with God, all things are possible; and therefore, *impossible is nothing*. That's right, nothing shall be impossible to them that believe.[9] So, do you believe?

Know today that it is possible for you to be successful, because you were made to prosper. You, my friend, were *made for more*. What more is there that you are seeking to achieve in your life? Whatever it is, you already have what it takes to do it! Because you are reading this book, I know that you already have a vision for your personal success, so now is the time to go forth and take the limits off your life. Take off your "mission-impossible shades." Although they may look cool on, they serve no purpose, and do you no good. Instead, try putting on your spiritual eyeglasses. In these glasses you'll see everything that you need on your journey to success, and when you see your success from this viewpoint, you will believe and know that *impossible is nothing*...**NO MATTER WHAT!**

---

[9] See Mark 9:23 KJV.

Winning Application

What glasses are you wearing today? Decide today that when you look at your life, you will look at it with all the fruit mentioned in today's reading. When you view life this way, exercising your faith in your own abilities and ambitions will become easier because you know that you have a great help in God.

Winning Ways Journal

Winning Quote

The spirit, the will to win, and the will to excel are the things that endure. These qualities are so much more important than the events that occur.

— **Vince Lombardi,** *American Football Coach*

Day-28

Find Your Will To Win

After you have taken the limits off yourself, as you were encouraged to do on yesterday, now it is time to find your personal *will to do* and *become* whatever you choose. It is time to find your *will to win*. I use again the sports analogy because it is a great example of will and perseverance in motion. One such example that stands out in my mind is the 2004 Summer Olympics. Almost every event in the competition was a true display of people finding the *will to win*.

The USA men's basketball team, for example, had been criticized and belittled because of the team's inability to qualify for the gold medal game. Although they had won the gold medal for the last 12 years, after sending NBA players, in 2004 the team barely qualified for the bronze game. Despite the shame the players felt and the ridicule they received for losing the gold medal, they still had one more game to play in hopes of redeeming themselves as great athletes. At best, they still had a chance at winning the bronze.

As I watched the game and listened to the commentators talk about the tragedy of the team's loss, I was overcome with empathy for the players, because I knew that inside them had been the will to win that gold medal. I was sure that the *will* – meaning the mental powers manifested as in *wishing, choosing, or desiring a thing to be so* – was there. The team had never lost the *will to win*. Yet with that will to win, they had been unable to bring home the gold.

As I continued to watch the game, the thought occurred to me that this same *will* the team had to win the gold had to be still there in order for them to try for the bronze. Their will didn't just die; it lived on in each of the players. This was demonstrated in the end when they took home the bronze medal in their final game. I rationalized about all of the reasons they could have used to justify giving up, but none of those things swayed them. It was their incessant, stubborn *will to win* that brought them back on to the court and crowned them victorious over the Lithuania team. Their will, their desire, and passion had kept them in the game, not just physically but mentally as well. At the end of the game, I could see the sweet look of victory on each of their faces, the corners of their mouths turned up into smiles, their eyes reflecting a much-needed relief. Relief that, despite what had happened in the previous games, they were not going home empty handed. They were still going home with a medal and a victory. This, I thought, was a great example of how each of us must respond when we face adversity. We must never lose the *will to win*. Daily, we must use our mental powers to will a thing to be so in our lives.

Whatever it is that you are striving to do in your life, it will not manifest itself to you and for you unless you go forth with *will*. Once you do this, like the US men's basketball team, you will find what you need to stay in the game. Or for that matter, to get back into the game when nothing seems to be going in your favor. In times like these, it is your will that will keep you sane in the midst of trying times and help you stay focused on your goal. It is certain that if you have no *will to win*, then win, you won't. But with your *will*, you have just what you need to make the most of every opportunity — win, lose, or draw. Today you must affirm that your *will to win*, when put into action, will cause you to be successful. Even when things are not going as you had planned, you must go inside your mind and find your personal *will to win*. There you will find that desire and passion that will cause you to stay in the game, and with it, you will win ...**NO MATTER WHAT!**

Winning Application

Have you found your *will to win*? Today, as you think about this question, identify a situation in your life when, in the face of adversity, you stood strong and enacted your will. Take a few moments to write this account down in your journal. Also, list other times when you enacted your will so that you can reflect on them later. Now, if you did it once, you can do it again! The next time you feel as if there is no hope, think back on those times as examples of what you are truly capable of accomplishing.

Winning Ways Journal

Winning Quote

I have learned in whatsoever state I am, therewith to be content.

- **Philippians 4:11,** *Holy Bible, KJV*

Day-29

Be Content in Every Season

Having a will to win is one thing, but being able to persevere during the good and the not-so-good times is another. If you have not discovered this already, you will find that success in life will come and go. There will be times when you will feel as if you are on top of the world. There will be other times when you will feel as if things are not moving as fast as, or in the direction, you want them to go. Simply put, these varying times may be considered the *seasons* of your success.

Recognizing seasons is important, for it is during each season, whether in harvest or drought, that you must learn to be *content*—content, not as in "satisfied," but *content* as in "thankful." You see, you do not always have to be satisfied with what you have or where you are, but it is important to remain thankful. Your situation may be compared to having a car that runs well, but has a few dents and needs a paint job. You're thankful for it because it takes you from point A to point B, but you still desire to someday have a car that looks good also. You want a car that not only gets you where you want to go but one that gets you there in style. It is not that you are content and willing to stay in the old car, but you are thankful, because you know that your harvest for a better one is just around the corner.

In your time of harvest, be grateful for the fruit that has been produced in your life. Pick your fruit wisely, use it wisely, and share it with those around you who have planted seeds in your life. In times of drought, focus on the beauty of your harvest, find a lesson in your season of drought, and grow through it and from it. Peace comes in understanding that your latter will be greater than what you are experiencing at the moment. This type of contentment will keep you from the moaning and groaning that can poison your mind and paralyze you on the road to success. Remember that it is how you handle your seasons of drought that will determine when and how well your harvest will come. Taking on a negative attitude will not only stop your harvest, but it can cut so deeply that it will destroy even the roots of success. Therefore, you must strive to keep a positive attitude; you must not be weary in where you are, but in every season you must be content.[10] Be thankful, knowing and believing that the work that you have put in today will become your harvest of tomorrow. Keep on plowing and planting...**NO MATTER WHAT!**

---

[10] See Gal. 6:9 and Phil. 4:11 KJV.

Winning Application

Understanding that there is a season for everything, including drought, begin to think about the people and things around you for which you are grateful right this moment. Count them and write a list of the ways that you are truly blessed on this day in your life. Tuck your list away in a safe place, and the next time you feel a drought season coming on, *water* your success "ground" with this list of things for which you are yet thankful, and watch your mind, your heart, and yes, even your season, begin to change.

Winning Ways Journal

Winning Quote

Without struggle there is no progress.

— **Fredrick Douglass,** *African American Abolitionist / Editor*

Day-30

Welcome the Struggle

It's been a long journey, but you've made it through all 30 days. You persevered until the end — some of you with ease, and others with a bit of struggle. On our final day, let's talk a bit about *the struggle*. I am speaking of the struggle that you have now, and maybe even the struggle you will have after you finish reading this book and start working to put your faith into action. Yesterday, we talked about the seasons of life, and *struggle* is one of them. Although struggle is one of the seasons that most of us would rather omit, unfortunately, we cannot. All of us must, at one time or another, experience struggle. Therefore, it is important to understand the role of struggle along the success journey.

Struggles come into our lives to help us develop strength, character, and other traits to equip us for life. Think what life would look like in the natural if we skipped seasons. What would we do without spring — a period of growth and development for plants and trees, but a period when vegetation is vulnerable to other elements of nature? What if we moved directly from summer to winter without experiencing fall? In some areas, without fall there would be no harvest.

When I think about successful people, it seems that those who have some of the best success stories have experienced some of the worst struggles. These people have weathered the storms of life and, in so doing, have achieved a great measure of success in life. You know their names — Oprah Winfrey, Nat King Cole, Martin Luther King, Jr.,

Stevie Wonder, and the list goes on and on. These people faced such adversities as rape, ridicule, disability, and humiliation; yet they rose from "the struggle" to stand on the shoulders of triumph. These once everyday people, now megastars, are just like all of us. While it is true that they are no different from you or me, there is one thing, however, that separates them from most people—their willingness to go through *the struggle*. It was through their struggles that they became victors. Had these people not overcome personal struggles, it is very likely that we would not even know their names today. Like millions of others, they would have faded into the dark shadows along with the other nameless, faceless people who did not make a difference in the world.

In spite of knowing the stories of how others rose to fame and success, most of us, if given a choice, would choose not to struggle. There is something in us that causes us to shy away from struggle. We *refuse* to struggle, especially if there is an easier way out of the dilemma in which we find ourselves. While it is true that no one likes to struggle, it is ever so clear that if you do not struggle, you will stay who you are and where you are. There will be little or no progress. It is *struggle* that builds character; it is *struggle* that changes you. To illustrate this, let's revisit the caterpillar. In the cocoon, if the caterpillar does not struggle to get out at the proper time, it will shrivel up and die, and will never know the joy of soaring through the air as the beautiful butterfly it was destined to become. As it beats its wings against the walls of the cocoon, the wings become stronger and stronger, getting ready for flight. You, my dear friend, in many ways, are just like that caterpillar, which emerged from the cocoon as a beautiful butterfly. You, too, were created to become someone special. In order to be that person you were destined to be, you must prepare yourself to fight for what you know is yours.

Although there may be a few things in life worth having that come easily, there is nothing of real value in life that comes without a price. Frederick Douglass said it best when he said, "Without struggle there is no progress." If you want to progress, you must learn how to go through struggle successfully. You see, if success were an easy road, the road would be crowded, because everyone would travel it. Instead, the road to success is reserved only for those who are exercising their "wings" to build strength, those who are willing to lift the kind of "weights" that help build spiritual muscles. The more muscles you build, the better able you will be to go through the struggle and to eventually overcome.

If you don't get anything else from this book, understand this one thing: if you truly want to be successful, then you must expect, and accept, that struggle will be a part of your journey. As you move closer to your goal, you will receive the revelation that the very thing you need in order to progress can be found *in the struggle*. If you need patience, you'll find it in the struggle. Do you need joy? It's in the struggle. Perseverance? You can find it in there — in the struggle. Whatever you need is in *the struggle*, but in order to receive that which you need, you *must* be willing to face every obstacle with the mind to overcome.

On this final day, here is my challenge to you. Whatever it is that you desire to be successful in or at — GO FOR IT! As you struggle toward your success, always remember that you are a butterfly in the making, so dream, struggle, progress, and ultimately soar...**NO MATTER WHAT!**

Winning Application

On this final day, I want to end by asking you to consider these three questions: What are your dreams? What are your struggles? How have you progressed through them in the past, and how will you do so in the future? Make the commitment today to examine these areas so that you won't become stuck in the struggle phase, and never progress.

Winning Ways Journal

Congratulations!

You made it! You have experienced thirty days of Winning Ways that will last you a lifetime. You deserve a great round of applause, a standing ovation, and a roaring "YEAH-H-H-H!" for having come this far. Through it all, you persevered and proved not only to me, but also to yourself, that you ARE destined for success! So now what? Now is the time to remember to apply what you have learned about yourself and your success. I challenge you in the days to come, to randomly select those topics that you found most beneficial to you. Review them so that you will not forget those Winning Ways that will be most essential to your success. Remember that it is through repetition and application that we truly learn and absorb things. Don't hesitate to put in the extra work to make sure that what you need "sinks in." This way you'll be better able to pull them from your mind and spirit when you find yourself faced with daily situations that can cause you to lose sight of your success.

Once again, congratulations on having completed the first thirty days of a *life full of success*. Come what may, always remember never to give up or give in…**NO MATTER WHAT!**

There's More To Come...

What Is the Winning Ways Book Series?

Designed as a quick read, the *Winning Ways* Book Series is one that can be read as a daily affirmation, devotion, or meditation to the testament that each of us can thrive in every aspect of life. The goal of the series is to empower you, to do more, be more, and achieve more in life. It provides you with techniques, ideas, principles and strategies to help you along the way.

What Are Winning Ways?

Winning Ways are techniques, ideas, principles, and strategies (T.I.P.S.) geared toward empowering readers to be successful in specific areas of their personal and professional lives. Much like nuggets of wisdom, *Winning Ways* are brief empowerment readings that will help to empower you on particular subject matters.

What Is the Format?

Each series is designed to be read daily in a thirty-day period. Each day consists of a **Winning Quote**, a **Winning Way** reading, and a **Winning Application** to actively apply the T.I.P.S. to the reader's life. Each book includes daily journal pages to record your thoughts and impressions throughout your journey.

Want more empowering titles from the Winning Ways Book Series?

To contact us, write to:

Winning Within
P.O. Box 7237
Kansas City, MO 64113

Email: info@ayannawebster.com
www.ayannawebster.com
1.866.WIN.4.WIN

About The Author

EXPERIENCE **A'Yanna Webster** and you're sure to experience a multi-talented force to be reckoned with! A talented speaker, coach, entrepreneur, and author, A'Yanna is using her God given talents to *empower, inspire, and uplift* audiences across the nation.

A'Yanna is the Founder and President of *Winning Within*, which provides speaking, training, and coaching services for groups and individuals.

As an entrepreneur, she has served as a trainer, speaker, and coach for a $2 million a year multi-level marketing company. She has partnered with more than 300 clients and business associates empowering them to achieve personal, financial, and physical success.

As a speaker, A'Yanna is a certified member of the Les Brown Speakers Network. She is also a contract speaker for Monster.com's *Making It Count Programs* and travels nationally motivating thousands of high schools and colleges students.

She is the host of the television talk show, *Winning Ways with A'Yanna Webster.*

A talented vocalist as well, her first Inspirational/Gospel CD is set to be released in 2007.

A'Yanna holds a Bachelors of Arts degree in Radio/TV Communications and a Masters of Public Affairs (MPA) with an emphasis in Non-Profit Management from Park University.

To schedule A'Yanna for your next event contact her at:

Winning Within
P.O. Box 7237
Kansas City, MO 64113
1.866.WIN.4.WIN

Email: info@ayannawebster.com
Website: www.ayannawebster.com